BREAK OUT
of POVERTY
into FINANCIAL
ABUNDANCE

SONYA L. THOMPSON
Foreword By Dr. Nasir Siddiki

Dedication

I dedicate this book to my Heavenly Father who was gracious enough to trust me with this assignment. Father, thank you for grafting me into the body of Christ and allowing me to be part of the kingdom. Thank you for sharing your heart with me each day. There is truly no one like you. Thank you for taking this vessel of clay and turning it into a vessel which can bring you glory. My life is totally and completely yielded to you and no one can ever take your place.

May the knowledge of your glory cover the earth as the waters cover the sea. May your kingdom come and your will be done on this earth as it is in heaven. May the anointing of your Spirit rise up from these pages to empower, prosper and encourage those who will hear your call to **"Break Out of Poverty Into Financial Abundance."**

Table of Contents

Acknowledgements

First, I want to thank my wonderful husband Chris for supporting my every venture. Thank you for embracing God's call on my life and for encouraging me to always do my best. Thank you for spending twenty-two beautiful years with me. I love you.

To my son Aaron, I love you and declare you will do great things for the kingdom of God. Allow Him to guide you on every turn. I see greatness in you.

Thanks to Pastor Tony McCoy for being my shepherd. You have a gift of drawing out the gifts of those you come into contact with. Thank you for taking time to instruct and correct me. I love you and am so thankful to God for sending me to Hope International.

Thank you to my First Lady, Pastor Jodie McCoy. You are a true "mood-setter" in the body of Christ. You have constantly encouraged and inspired me. Thank you for speaking a blessing into my life on so many occasions. I love you and am honored to have you as my First Lady.

I also would like to thank Dr. Tom Leding for his encouragement and guidance every week. Thank you for reminding me to keep my eyes on Jesus. You are a diamond in the rough. The world desperately needs to hear the message God has placed in you.

Dr. Siddiki, thank you for taking time to pour into my life. Your hunger for the Word and ways of God are an inspiration to me. Your anointing has touched my life in such a profound way that I will never be the same again. May the Father continue to open doors for you and pour out His favor upon you.

Foreword

Sonya has done a great job with this book! She breaks down the reasons why the church is in a state of lack, how to turn that around and become the blessing we were always meant to be.

Your life will be transformed as you read and apply God's principles in this book. Remember, you are not just to change your life, but to change your world.

The church needs to learn that money is a tool to get God's work done on the earth – to take His Kingdom all over the earth. The church is God's vessel to demonstrate His love and bring His blessings to the world. How can this happen when we do not understand our role to prosper or even apply His principles to bring prosperity to us?

As you apply these principles you will not only change your world, but you will become the blessing God always planned for you to be.

Dr Nasir Siddiki
www.wisdomministries.org

Introduction

I attended a conference not long ago and watched as everyone was jumping, dancing and praising God. It was a beautiful sight. After the speaker delivered her message she began to prepare us to give an offering. A holy hush came over the crowd. I could literally feel the tension in the atmosphere. It felt like someone had sucked the air out of the room and everyone was holding their breath. There is something terribly wrong with this picture. We're free when it comes to praising, crying and jumping but are "locked up" in the prison of poverty in the area of our finances because we refuse to give.

Hosea 4:6 says

My people are destroyed from lack of knowledge. "Because you have rejected knowledge, I also reject you as my priests; because you have ignored the law of your God, I also will ignore your children."

There are more men and women of God teaching on financial prosperity than ever before, yet we are still perishing. So what is the cause? We have rejected knowledge. We believe we can break out of poverty another way. I am here to tell you it will never happen. The Kingdom of God is a seed based kingdom. Everything comes through the process of sowing and reaping. Until we realize this, we'll keep jumping and shouting and still be broke. Praise is not the seed for financial increase. Begging and crying are not the seed for financial increase. **Genesis 1:11** says every seed produces after its own kind. Money is the only seed you can sow to produce financial increase.

The body of Christ has been given a divine commission and mandate to carry the gospel of the kingdom all over the earth. In order to do this, it will take a lot of money. It's also going to take a remnant of people who will listen to the voice of the Holy Spirit and receive the knowledge of kingdom principles for financial increase. I believe with all of my heart God is raising up a financial army for this end time harvest. He is putting together a group of sons who will be led by the Spirit to distribute the money wherever He directs them to send it. They will give without holding their breath. This army won't just dance and shout, but will prove their love by their obedience in giving. If you are a part of this army, then you are reading the right book at the right time! This is your divine appointment. Based on my experience I can assure you, your life will never be the same as you subject your finances to the government of God.

The Holy Spirit has breathed life into the words on these pages. May He speak to your heart and show you the way of escape. Like Paul, I pray the eyes of your understanding will be enlightened. May you gain revelation on how to skillfully use the keys of the kingdom to Break out of Poverty into Financial Abundance!

Chapter 1

Who Do You Really Trust?

Before you can even begin to break out of financial captivity, you must first settle the "trust" issue in the area of finances. I'm certain if I conducted a survey with one hundred born again believers and asked if they trusted God, one hundred percent would respond with a definite, resounding yes! Now if this is true, if one hundred percent of believers really trust the Father, then why aren't one hundred percent of believers around the nation tithing? Why are we still wrestling in this area? Even more so, many believers and preachers go to such great lengths to convince themselves and others the tithe is a practice under the Law, when Scripture clearly shows this is not the case. When we really get down to it, the real heart of the matter is not the Law or grace, Old Testament or New Testament; it really boils down to a matter of trust.

I speak to believers frequently in the area of finances. They get their budget together and tell me how they are struggling financially, trying to make it. They say they really want to tithe but know God understands they must pay their bills and take care of their family. What God really understands is He is not trusted by the individual. I know this sounds insensitive and almost outrageous, but it's the truth. When they tell me they know God understands their situation, I usually ask them a few questions to consider in an effort to resolve their situation.

First I ask them, if they believe they are saved and will be with the Lord when they leave this earth. Of course they say yes! Then I ask, " How can you trust your eternal soul with a God whom you have never seen but can't trust Him with your money"? At this question a blank stare usually comes across their face. They realize they are convinced by the witness of the Holy Spirit- whom they have never seen, that they are born again and will be going to heaven when they leave this earth. If I can add, no one can talk them out of the promise of eternal life through Jesus Christ. It's like the older folks say, "I know that I know". Don't you think a soul is more costly to God than your money? I am totally convinced beyond a shadow of a doubt, it takes a whole lot more faith to trust God for eternal salvation than to believe for financial provision. For some reason this is not the case in the body of Christ today. The Bible tells us the price for a soul is costly and its ransom can't be paid.

Look at what is recorded in Psalm 49

Those who trust in their wealth And boast in the multitude of their riches, None of them can by any means redeem his brother, Nor give to God a ransom for him For the redemption of their souls is costly, And it shall cease forever

—(Psalm 49:6-8 NKJV)

The Hebrew definition of the word wealth in this text is **chayil.** A few of the words used to describe wealth in this definition are: force of men or means, power, strength or ability.

As Christians we tend to comfort ourselves by applying this Scripture to the ungodly that are rich in this world's substance, because it takes the pressure off of us. There are a whole lot of people who are in abject poverty or struggling from one paycheck to the next, who trust in their own force, means, power and ability. This is the primary reason why there is such great difficulty for the body of Christ to trust the Father with their financial resources. We continue to try and prosper by our own hands, our own force and means, but it's not working! As a result we are in "toiling" mode, trying to make ends meet. We are working two to three jobs, seven days a week, double overtime, etc. As we continue to operate in this manner, we ignore the kingdom principles of prosperity and put our trust in the work of our hands. As a result we are suffering tremendously in the area of finances.

If you have difficulty returning the tithe and giving an offering, I have to ask you again, who do you really trust?

One of the main questions I get from those who do not tithe and give is, "how will I be able to pay bills if I tithe? I can barely make it now"! I understand this reasoning because the person has factual obligations staring him/her in the face. Creditors are calling, the rent is due, the baby needs a new pair of shoes and so on. The facts are real, but allow me for a moment to impart some truth into your spirit that will set you free if you can receive it. Everything withdrawn from the kingdom must come by **faith**. If tithing and giving was going to be easy the Father wouldn't have invited His people to prove or "test" Him in Malachi chapter three. He already knew these questions and concerns would come into play. He already knew the struggle His people would face. To reassure us, the Father makes several grandeur promises in Malachi chapter three of how He will literally bless our socks off when we obey Him.

Bring ye all the tithes into the storehouse, that there may be meat in mine house, and prove me now herewith, saith the Lord of hosts, <u>if I will not open you the windows of heaven, and pour you out a blessing, that there shall not be room enough to receive it</u>. And I will rebuke the devourer for your sakes, and he shall not destroy the fruits of your ground; neither shall your vine cast her fruit before the time in the field, saith the Lord of hosts. And all nations shall call you blessed: for ye shall be a delightsome land, saith the Lord of hosts.

—(Malachi 3:10-12 KJV)

Failure to understand the benefits of the tithe is the main reason why believers are fearful of trusting God with their finances. Our lack of a clear understanding of the Father's intent for this portion of Scripture causes us not to trust Him. What does He really mean in Malachi chapter three? We will explore this further in the next few chapters. To the degree we understand the Word of God in this area will determine the degree of trust we have and the level of financial manifestation we walk in. Trust always ties back to the character of an individual. I'm sure you have a person or people in your life you trust. You trust them because they have proven by past behavior, they will perform as promised. Surely God is no less trustworthy than mere man!

David said this about trusting in God.

Those who know your name trust in you, for you, Lord, have never forsaken those who seek you.
— **(Psalm 9:10 NIV)**

Those who **know** the character of God, nature of God and authority they have in His name can trust in Him. This knowledge can only be obtained by experience. A person who has operated in and experienced the character, nature and authority of God can fully and truly say they trust in Him. In other words, they have seen the results for themselves. It's God's nature to bless, to give and love his children. Your Heavenly Father's character is impeccable. No one has ever proven His Word to be false. If the Word isn't working, it's not God's fault. I am sure you can think of many instances in your life where He showed Himself faithful. If God is lying about the financial principles in the Bible, then everything else has to be a lie. We'll have to throw the whole book out. But, I am confident this is not the case.

Numbers 23:19 has become an anchor for my soul concerning the Father's nature.

God is <u>not a man</u>, that he should lie; neither the son of man, that he should repent: hath he said, and shall he not do it? or hath he spoken, and shall he not make it good?
— **(Numbers 23:19 KJV)**

We can't compare God to men. It's not a matter of God not lying; He just CAN'T lie! Anything He speaks must come to pass. If He is lying about financial abundance, He is also lying about your salvation and everything else in the Bible. We have to get to a point where we accept all of the Word of God not part of it. We may not literally tear pages and promises out of the Bible in the natural, but from a spiritual standpoint that's exactly what we do when we reject the truth of His Word. The Word of God is the whole truth and nothing but the truth. Let **Numbers 23:19** take root in your heart today. Declare it every chance you get, to remind yourself in whom you have placed your eternal soul and in whose hands you have placed your financial future.

Here is another reference which is worth a close look.

Praise ye the Lord. Blessed is the man that feareth the Lord, that delighteth greatly in his commandments.

21

His seed shall be mighty upon earth: the generation of the upright shall be blessed. Wealth and riches shall be in his house: and his righteousness endureth for ever. Unto the upright there ariseth light in the darkness: he is gracious, and full of compassion, and righteous. A good man sheweth favour, and lendeth: he will guide his affairs with discretion. Surely he shall not be moved for ever: the righteous shall be in everlasting remembrance. He shall not be afraid of evil tidings: his heart is fixed, trusting in the Lord. His heart is established, he shall not be afraid, until he see his desire upon his enemies. He hath dispersed, he hath given to the poor; his righteousness endureth for ever; his horn shall be exalted with honour. The wicked shall see it, and be grieved; he shall gnash with his teeth, and melt away: the desire of the wicked shall perish.

— (Psalm 112:1-10 KJV)

The Psalmist says wealth and riches are in the house of the man or woman who fears the Lord (hates evil). His heart is fixed **TRUSTING** in the Lord. Your heart must be at a point where it is fixed- steadfast, unmovable and anchored concerning the character, nature and Word of the Father in the area of finances. Trusting is a continuous action. You don't trust one day and walk in fear the next. That's a wishy-washy relationship to say the least. The one who actively trusts the Lord has a heart that's fixed.

No matter what the circumstances may be screaming in your ear, your heart must stay fixed trusting in the Lord.

If you intend to break out of poverty into financial abundance, it's time to settle the fact today that the Father says what He means and means what He says. Don't let anyone explain away the truth of the Word of God. God really means what He says. The same God who saved your soul is the very same God who has equipped you to break out of your financial prison today, if you trust Him and put His financial principles to work.

Chapter 2

It's Available For You

I would like to dedicate this chapter to those who believe financial abundance is available for others but have a problem receiving it for themselves.

In Luke chapter fifteen there's one statement which changed my entire life. I would like to take a moment to share the scriptural account which deals with the prodigal son. We pick up in the text at a point where the prodigal son has returned home and they have a major celebration for him.

"Meanwhile, the older son was in the field. When he came near the house, he heard music and dancing. So he called one of the servants and asked him what was going on.

'Your brother has come,' he replied, 'and your father has killed the fattened calf because he has him back safe and sound.' "The older brother became angry and refused to go in. So his father went out and pleaded with him. But he answered his father, 'Look! All these years I've been slaving for you and never disobeyed your orders. Yet you never gave me even a young goat so I could celebrate with my friends. But when this son of yours who has squandered your property with prostitutes comes home, you kill the fattened calf for him!' "'My son,' the father said, 'you are always with me, and everything I have is yours'.

— (Luke 15:25-31 NIV)

Take note of the words in verse thirty-one, "everything I have is yours". The Father was talking to the son who was always with him, who obeyed him and honored him. This son did what his father required of him, but he never received a "party" like the younger brother. He didn't know it, but he could have had a party at any time. This elder son wasn't aware of the access he had to his inheritance or the covenant he had with his father.

God's children are the same way today. We serve the Lord with all of or heart but fail to realize we have access to everything He has. Like the elder son, we get discouraged because it looks like everyone else seems to prosper except us! I used to think being wealthy was just for pastors. I figured God had to prosper them because they were called to preach the Gospel, but I found out there were a lot of broke preachers too! Not only were they broke but they were standing at the pulpit Sunday after Sunday teaching their congregants that being broke was holy and acceptable to God.

I attended a church in Virginia many years ago and the pastor told us God was not obligated to give us anything beyond our needs. There is some truth to this. God is not obligated, but that's not the nature of our Father. Because of this teaching many people look for just enough. As long as their bills are paid, they figure everything is alright. This is not our God! He is a God of abundance and overflow. Everything He touches has a fingerprint of abundance on it!

Look again at verse thirty-one. This time I want you to imagine the Father speaking directly to you. See Him telling you everything He has is available to you! Put your name at the end of this statement, " Everything the Father has is _____". Don't allow yourself to walk in a limited, just enough, lack and barely getting by mentality another day! Avoid the temptation of basing your status on what you have available or what you can produce, rather than what the Father says He has available for you.

Get Rid Of The Competition

Like the elder son, we think we must compete for this world's riches. Often times we will find ourselves in competition with members of the body of Christ. We wonder why God gave them the new car or house when they just got saved six months ago! We try to qualify our worthiness to the Father like the elder son; but we fail to realize when we do this, we put our brothers and sisters on a lower level than we are. Comparison and justifying sends a message to the Father that we are better and deserve what they have more than they do. In the beginning the Father created the heavens and the earth. He is the one who placed all the rich substance on this earth , so there's enough for everyone.

He is an infinite God who has an infinite supply of wealth. That's why He has the right to declare everything He has is yours. I want you to say this, **"All the Father has is mine. It's available for me now and I willingly receive from him by faith".** You are an heir and a joint heir with the Lord Jesus Christ. Heirs inherit things. Of course you have a spiritual inheritance as well. There's no doubt about that but you also have some "stuff" the Father wants to give you". If it belongs to Jesus, it belongs to you.

Look at these Scriptures,

The earth is the Lord's, and everything in it, the world, and all who live in it;

— (Psalm 24:1 NIV)

Jehovah speaking to Cyrus; See him speaking to you.

I will give you hidden treasures, riches stored in secret places, so that you may know that I am the Lord, the God of Israel, who summons you by name.

— (Isaiah 45:3 NIV)

Your Father knows where everything is because He put it here just for you. It's hidden for you but not from you. It's hidden for a time when you begin to accept and lay hold of His promises for yourself and your household. There's enough for everyone. There's no scarcity or lack in the kingdom of God, neither is there need for competition.

Let me share another text with you. This is one of my favorite. Our assistant pastor taught a Bible study a few years ago and he began to make a plea from the Father based on thess verses. As I read these verses I am reminded of that Wednesday evening Bible study when I was set free in the spirit of my mind. It came at a perfect time for me when I was feeling downright dejected and frustrated because I was dealing with what appeared to be a financial mountain.

Look at this verse with me.

What, then, shall we say in response to these things? If God is for us, who can be against us? He who did not spare his own Son, but gave him up for us all—how will he not also, along with him, graciously give us all things?
— (Romans 8:31- 32 NIV)

My Bible says He did not spare His own Son but gave Him up for us all; and along with Him, the Father graciously added "all things" to the package.

Do you know what the definition of all is? Yes, everything! What in the world would make you think your Father will withhold anything from you? In the King James this text says **in** Christ He has "freely" given us all things. In other words, it's yours for the taking, just receive by faith. When you received Christ, you received everything. There is nothing left for God to give you. Hasn't the Father already proven He is a bona fide giver? He gave up His Son and made eternal life available for you. You received Him freely now receive your abundance and all the rich substance the Father has set aside for you. Get this verse in your spirit. Meditate on it until it takes root in your heart and mind. Begin to declare on a daily basis, "Everything the Father has is mine!"

Chapter 3

What Are You Focusing On?

Maintaining a point of reference or focus will prove to be a key to break out of poverty into financial abundance. When you focus on something all of your attention is concentrated or converged on it. In Numbers chapter thirteen, God told Moses to send out some men to explore the land of Canaan. This was the promise land which flowed with milk and honey. When they went up to see the land, they found things just as God had described it, but ten spies decided to focus their attention on something other than the Father's report.

They came back to Moses and Aaron and the whole Israelite community at Kadesh in the Desert of Paran. There they reported to them and to the whole assembly

and showed them the fruit of the land. They gave Moses this account: "We went into the land to which you sent us, and it does flow with milk and honey! Here is its fruit. But the people who live there are powerful, and the cities are fortified and very large. We even saw descendants of Anak there.

— (Numbers 13:26-28 NIV)

But the men who had gone up with him said, "We can't attack those people; they are stronger than we are." And they spread among the Israelites a bad report about the land they had explored. They said, "The land we explored devours those living in it. All the people we saw there are of great size. We saw the Nephilim there (the descendants of Anak come from the Nephilim). We seemed like grasshoppers in our own eyes, and we looked the same to them."

— (Numbers 13:31-33 NIV)

Everything was just like God told them, but as you can see He left out a major detail- the Nephilim! These were men of old, renowned men- giants. Isn't that just like God? He tells you all of the good stuff but leaves out the challenges which must be faced in order to possess the land. Even though they had seen the land which flowed with milk and honey, even though it literally took two men with a large branch to carry back the fruit, they could not shift their focus away from the Nephilim. They focused on them for so long they began to view themselves as nothing. They literally began to see themselves as insignificant, small and powerless men of God.

This runs parallel to the body's Christ. We want to break out of poverty; we know the Father has so many wonderful promises in His word **BUT**, we keep looking at the debt and financial obligations until it becomes a "giant" in our lives. We have allowed ourselves and God to become small in comparison to the financial "giants" we face. Our focus has shifted from God's Word to our circumstances. Listen to me for a moment, what you focus on you will become. Let me say it another way, whatever you meditate on tells your spirit what you want to manifest in your life. Here's a text the Holy Spirit uncovered for me many years ago.

After Rachel gave birth to Joseph, Jacob said to Laban, "Send me on my way so I can go back to my own homeland. Give me my wives and children, for whom I have served you, and I will be on my way. You know how much work I've done for you." But Laban said to him, "If I have found favor in your eyes, please stay. I have learned by divination that the Lord has blessed me because of you." He added, "Name your wages, and I will pay them." Jacob said to him, "You know how I have worked for you and how your

livestock has fared under my care. The little you had before I came has increased greatly, and the Lord has blessed you wherever I have been. But now, when may I do something for my own household?" "What shall I give you?" he asked. "Don't give me anything," Jacob replied. "But if you will do this one thing for me, I will go on tending your flocks and watching over them: Let me go through all your flocks today and remove from them every speckled or spotted sheep, every dark-colored lamb and every spotted or speckled goat. They will be my wages. And my honesty will testify for me in the future, whenever you check on the wages you have paid me. Any goat in my possession that is not speckled or spotted, or any lamb that is not dark-colored, will be considered stolen." "Agreed," said Laban. "Let it be as you have said." That same day he removed all the male goats that were streaked or spotted, and all the speckled or spotted female goats (all that had white on them) and all the dark-colored lambs, and he placed them in the care of his sons. Then he put a three-day journey between himself and Jacob, while Jacob continued to tend the rest of Laban's flocks. Jacob, however, took fresh-cut branches from poplar, almond and plane trees and made white stripes on them by peeling the bark and exposing the white inner wood of the branches. Then he placed the peeled branches in all the watering troughs, so that they would be directly in front of the flocks when they came to

drink. When the flocks were in heat and came to drink, they mated in front of the branches. And they bore young that were streaked or speckled or spotted.

— (Genesis 30:25-39 NIV)

Now this might be a bit extreme because we are talking about animals, but notice in the next chapter Jacob shares with Laban how he received this revelation - How his flocks became whatever he wanted them to be.

"In breeding season I once had a dream in which I looked up and saw that the male goats mating with the flock were streaked, speckled or spotted. The angel of God said to me in the dream, 'Jacob.' I answered, 'Here I am.' And he said, 'Look up and see that all the male goats mating with the flock are streaked, speckled or spotted, for I have seen all that Laban has been doing to you".

— (Genesis 31:10-12 NIV)

If this principle can work for animals what do you think will happen to you if you make a life changing decision to focus on the Father's promises concerning your financial prosperity? What do you think would happen if you decided to put images of wealth, financial freedom, abundance and overflow before your eyes and stopped focusing on the so called giant of debt, lack and insufficiency? Even more so, focus on Jesus who is the author and finisher of your faith. He was able to keep his focus on the cross because of the joy set before Him. You have to see the end from the beginning and the beginning from the end, if you're going to break free.

The Bible says as a man thinks in his heart so is he. What you focus on, what you set your affections on, you will ultimately become. So put those bills away and stop trying to make a dollar out of fifty cents. Get your focus back on the Father and what the He has promised you in His Word. Become what His Word says you're supposed to be.

Watch Out For Fear

Let's take this a step further and look at the life of Job for a moment. Men and women of God take the life of Job as a "cop out" to say <u>God</u> put Job through the most horrific test of his life. Many sermons and songs have been penned from Job, of how God gives and takes away.

Let's look at the events that led up to his test.

For the thing <u>which I greatly feared</u> is come upon me, and that which I was afraid of is come unto me.

— (Job 3:25 KJV)

The words above are from the mouth of Job not from God. Here is something to consider, fear has a voice. When people fear something, they express those fears with words- either to someone or to themselves. I will bet my bottom dollar Job voiced his fears and Satan heard him. Further, **Proverbs 6:2** says we are ensnared by the words of our mouth. Many times the traps we find ourselves in have come from our own mouth. Let's back up a chapter and see what happens as Satan goes before God.

Again there was a day when the sons of God came to present themselves before the Lord, and Satan came also among them to present himself before the Lord. And the Lord said unto Satan, From whence comest thou? And Satan answered the Lord, and said, From going to and fro in the earth, and from walking up and down in it. And the Lord said unto Satan, Hast thou considered my servant Job, that there is none like him in the earth, a perfect and an upright man, one that feareth God, and escheweth evil? and still he holdeth fast his integrity, although thou movedst me against him, to destroy him without cause.

— (Job 2:1-3 KJV)

God asked Satan where he had been. Now you and I both know God knew where Satan was coming from since He is omnipresent-everywhere at all times. Don't you know God knew Satan was coming to Him to accuse Job? Satan had a legal right to accuse Job based on what we read in **Job 3:25 - that which he feared had come upon him**. This was the reason God asked him have you considered my servant Job. You might be reading this and say, this is heresy. "I have never heard that before." Can you show me another instance where God strips everything away from one of His sons. Anytime we see devastating loss in the lives of men or women of God it's usually because of their own words, acts of disobedience or failure to follow instruction. That's hard for us to accept. We want God to take the fall for all of our trouble but we have more control over our life than we think. Of course I realize we will face difficulty in life, which is not of our own doing because we live in a sinful world. You may say Paul went through a lot for the Gospel. He was shipwrecked, beaten, bit by a snake, and put in prison. Yes, this is true , it was for the **Gospel**, but he was delivered from it all. The Psalmist said,

Many are the afflictions of the righteous: but the Lord delivereth him out of them all.

— (Psalm 34:19-KJV)

Satan gains legal access through your words and actions which are contrary to the will and purposes of God. I will say this again, fear has a voice. Job's greatest fear became a reality because at one point he voiced it and Satan heard him. God watches over his word to perform it (**Jeremiah 1:12**) and Satan watches over his word- **fear**, to perform it as well. He is the one who comes to **steal, kill and destroy- (John 10:10**), if he can gain legal access into your life through your words or acts of disobedience.

God wasn't out to destroy Job. Nor is He out to destroy you. He's not a God who gives and takes away. He's not an Indian giver. Those were Job's words, spoken in the midst of the most difficult time of his life. If you follow the book of Job to the end you will find out he received double for his trouble. If God was interested in destroying Job why would He restore twice as much as he had before? It doesn't add up.

Your Father loves you so much. You are not a pawn on a chess board. He doesn't play games with Satan in order to teach you a lesson. This is not scriptural. God trains us and teaches us through His word. Your ability to break out of poverty into financial abundance has everything to do with what you believe about your Father and what y o u focus on. Don't allow fear of the unknown or impending circumstances to cause you to shift your focus from the promises of God.

Chapter 4

Prosperity Starts Within

Prospering in your soul, your mind, will and emotions, is a very important piece of the financial pie. As a society we are taught to spend most of our time focusing on external things to create wealth. One of the major areas of our focus is education. We spend most of our lives on a quest to become "intelligent" in the eyes of men. We are taught early on to get a good education so we can get a good job and make a good living. As a result, all of our attention has shifted to external sources to create wealth, but true creation of wealth starts from within. Secular education does prosper us mentally, but only on a secular level. There are no schools teaching our children how to prosper according to God's Word. Plus, there are only a handful of Christian schools which teach in the area of finances and stewardship. We are getting taught a lot of information and have tremendous skills, but many college graduates are still broke! I know a millionaire and several other very financially prosperous people who never went to college. Let me make it clear, I am NOT anti-education. I have a college degree, but I understand a college degree isn't going to make me wealthy. This is the deception we have been led to believe for years, but statistics have proven otherwise. Education is great, but it's not the key to financial abundance. Secular schools prepare you to take your talents and gifts to the secular world. Our soul needs a different type of education in order to take wealth out of the world and bring it into the kingdom.

Here are a few statements to consider: Your wealth file is an internal not an external occurrence. Your current financial status is a manifestation of your internal prosperity.

John wrote to the church and told us under the inspiration of the Holy Spirit, to prosper and be in health in accordance with the prosperity of our soul.

Beloved, I wish above all things that thou mayest prosper and be in health, even as thy soul prospereth.

— (3 John 1:2 KJV)

Wait a minute! John said we would prosper and be in health even as our **SOUL** prospers. This would explain why some people are more prosperous than others; we manifest financial abundance based on what we have deposited in our wealth file- our **soul**. Whatever has been sown in the soul must manifest externally.

Galatians six sheds some additional light in this area.

Be not deceived; God is not mocked: for whatsoever a man soweth, that shall he also reap.

— (Galatians 6:7 KJV)

This verse above says "whatever you sow, you will reap". You can't pull out of the natural realm what has not been sown in the spiritual. Your outward financial manifestation is just an indication of what you have been sowing in your soul over the last few days, months and years. If you don't sow financial seed from the Word of God in your heart and mind, then you can't reap financial abundance. You see how it works?

First you must go to your bag of seed- the Word of God and find out what it says about wealth and abundance. Once you plant the Word in your soul, then you'll be on the right track to creating a life of abundance.

It's Time To Meditate

When I used to hear the word meditate I would associate it with New Age and Mysticism. Meditation is a Biblical practice which the world has pretty much stolen right from under us. They use this practice **without God**- chanting and humming and so forth connecting with their "inner self". As Christians, when we mediate, it must be on the Word of God.

This book of the law shall not depart out of thy mouth; but thou shalt meditate therein day and night, that thou mayest observe to do according to all that is written therein: for then thou shalt make thy way prosperous, and then thou shalt have good success.

— (Joshua 1:8 KJV)

God told Joshua to meditate on the Word day and night, to do it and he would make himself prosperous. So you may ask, " How do I meditate on Scripture"? The word meditate means to utter, speak or muse over (absorb one's thoughts). This is meditation God's way. It's not just reading a verse and going on about your business. No, it's talking to yourself about it and rolling it over and over in your mind. You talk to yourself anyway so you might as well make it productive. This is a far cry from what we have been taught. We have been taught to memorize and quote Scriptures. There's no power in just quoting and memorizing Scriptures. I know this is true because I used to do it without any manifestation. True meditation has actions which follow, as evidenced in **Joshua 1:8**. God told Joshua to be careful to do- to do what? What he had meditated on!

I bet you know some folks who seemingly can finish a verse as soon as you start quoting it. But I have one simple question, where is the revelation and demonstration of the power of the Holy Spirit in our finances? We have proven for decades scripture quoting without revelation will not work. The Word has to move from your mental faculties, into your heart, then to the natural realm. It must come alive in you; then your financial situation will be resurrected the same way Jesus was resurrected from the dead. He is the living Word and He lives on the inside of you. Everything the Living Word touches must come alive and be restored, including your finances!

When you meditate on lack and limitation you allow the world to form your thoughts. I have to ask you the same question God asked Adam after he found out he was naked. God asked Adam "who told you that?" So I ask you, "who told you, you would never be debt free? Who told you paycheck to paycheck living is your lifestyle? Who told you minimum wage was all you can aspire to"? It's time to mediate on the prosperous truths of the Word of God and allow Him/them, to reshape your financial future. Mediating on the Word of God is an essential key to break out of poverty into financial abundance.

The Mind A Force To Be Reckoned With

God said He has wonderful thoughts and plans for our future, so let's find out what happened. Here's what the Father says about you,

"For I know the plans I have for you," declares the Lord, "plans to prosper you and not to harm you, plans to give you hope and a future."

— (Jeremiah 29:11 NIV)

Man was created in the image and likeness of God. We were created to think like God thinks, but our mind became skewed and distorted in the book of Genesis when Adam and Eve decided to partake of the tree of the knowledge of good and evil.

The Hebrew word for evil is **Rah**. It means to become spoiled or good for nothing. It also means to have thoughts of affliction, calamity, distress, mischief, sorrow or wickedness. Now we can plainly see why God warned Adam and Eve not to eat from the tree of the knowledge of good and evil. As a result of their disobedience, Adam and Eve's thought life and the thought life of all mankind became totally corrupted. Today we still wrestle with the effects of this one act of treason but there is good news! If we did not know any better, this mental illness would seem terminal and hopeless, but I found some good news in the Word of God.

But thanks be to God! He gives us the victory through our Lord Jesus Christ.

— (1 Corinthians 15:57 NIV)

During the week of passion, Jesus bled in seven areas. One of the areas w h e r e He shed his blood redeemed us from "evil" thoughts. When the crown of thorns was placed upon Jesus' head, piercing his scalp, it was at that moment man's mental prosperity was restored. We no longer have to be captivated by thoughts of evil. Through the blood of Jesus Christ, we now have the ability and authority to take every thought captive to the obedience of Christ. Look at what Paul said in **2 Corinthians**.

Casting down imaginations, and every high thing that exalteth itself against the knowledge of God, and bringing into captivity every thought to the obedience of Christ;
— (2 Corinthians 10:5 KJV)

Exercising this authority isn't automatic. It looks like you have to interactively and purposely process your thoughts. This verse also proves you and I have the power to recognize, capture and cast down an evil thought before it has an opportunity to take residence in our heart.

We have been introduced to a world of evil and as a result, if we will allow it, our mind can be shaped by information which has no place in the heart and mind of men and women of God. **Romans12:2** tells us not to allow the world to form or shape our thought patterns.

Do not conform to the pattern of this world, but be transformed by the renewing of your mind. Then you will be able to test and approve what God's will is—his good, pleasing and perfect will.
— (Romans 12:2 NIV)

The word transformed in the Greek is metamorphoo. It comes from **meta** which means to change after being with and **morphoo** which means changing form with inner reality. Your mind is properly changed only after it has been renewed with the truth of the Word of God- after your inner man has been with Him. How? In this case, by meditating on kingdom financial principles and allowing them to transform your mind in the area of finances.

There Is Only One Cure

The Word of God is the *ONLY* way to restore your thoughts to their original "Edenic" state. We look at and hear so much negative information during the course of a day, that's why it's imperative to meditate on the Word. Don't let people fool you into thinking positive affirmations are enough. Your mind must be washed daily with the water of the Word.

I spend a lot of time reading, listening to and studying the Word of God. I even sleep with my IPod headphones in my ears all night, playing Scriptures or lessons on financial increase. One time someone told me I was being brainwashed and I said, "You think"? Now the world has most of the body of Christ brainwashed into thinking their job, 401k plan and overtime are their financial source. We tremble at the thought of losing or walking away from our job even if God Himself tells us to do it because we see the job as our source and not the Father. My thought on being brainwashed is this: If I am going to be brainwashed, it might as well be by my Heavenly Father! After all I am supposed to think like Him.

Your financial future starts from within and the only cure for the disease of mental poverty is to take the medicine of the Word of God every single day- several times per day. In 2010 the Lord had me record a CD called **"Seeds of Prosperity".** It's a compilation of Scriptures "ministered"- spoken by myself, under the anointing of the Holy Spirit. The CD was designed to allow a person to listen to financial prosperity Scriptures during their down time. They could medicate and meditate on the Word of God, thus, renewing their mind in the area of financial prosperity. The Lord didn't tell me to teach anything on the CD, just minister the Word, because there is life in the Word all by itself. **Hebrews 4:12** says the Word of God is **"living and active."** As a result of people listening to the CD, I received many testimonies from individuals of how the Word began to speak to their heart and open up the eyes of their spiritual understanding to God's world of abundance.

It's so important to get control of this area before you can break out of poverty into abundance. Further, I hope you will embrace the Word as your only source of healing for the mental disease of poverty. Prosperity starts from within.

Your current financial situation whether good or bad is simply a result of yesterday's thought processes. Whatever you have been meditating on has finally made its way from the unseen world into the one which is seen.

Chapter 5

The Tongue- Who Can Tame This Crazy Thing?

Now that we have gotten the mind under control, let's deal with one of the most profound yet powerful members of the human body -the tongue. It's a small unsightly member, but it literally has the power to change the course of your life, for better or worse. Look at what Solomon recorded in Proverbs concerning the tongue.

Death and life are in the power of the tongue: and they that love it shall eat the fruit thereof.

— (Proverbs 18:21 KJV)

Life as you know it will change drastically, dramatically and almost instantly if this truth is planted in your heart. The tongue has accompanied many believers down the road to lack and insufficiency. Here's the reason why: Anything not used for its intended purpose will always produce undesirable results. For example, if I stick my finger in an electrical socket, the outcome can potentially be fatal. Why? Because my finger stuck in the socket is not the original intent and use of my finger or the socket. It's no different with the tongue. The tongue was never set in place to speak a report contrary to the Word of God. Many believers are "shocked' by the current state of their finances because they are sticking their finger in a socket every time their mouth is opened with a negative, contrary and evil financial report. This isn't the proper use of the tongue and has proven to produce fatal results for many believers.

As I look at Proverbs 18:21, I see a universal law which has been applied to the tongue- the tongue will produce fruit. Where does fruit come from? Seed of course. The universal law I am talking about is sowing and reaping. Sowing and reaping applies to everything you do in life. Every time you open your mouth you're sowing a word seed which will go out into the atmosphere and bring back a package. It's similar to placing an order on line and sitting back until UPS delivers it. Now don't get surprised when your delivery shows up and it's just what you ordered- lack, limitation, not enough or just enough! You better believe your tongue will deliver whatever financial future you order.

A look at James sheds some additional light on the power of the tongue.

The tongue also is a fire, a world of evil among the parts of the body. It corrupts the whole body, sets the whole course of one's life on fire, and is itself set on fire by hell. All kinds of animals, birds, reptiles and sea creatures are being tamed and have been tamed by mankind, but no human being can tame the tongue. It is a restless evil, full of deadly poison. With the tongue we praise our Lord and Father, and with it we curse human beings, who have been made in God's likeness. Out of the same mouth come praise and cursing. My brothers and sisters, this should not be. Can both fresh water and salt water flow from the same spring? My brothers and sisters, can a fig tree bear olives, or a grapevine bear figs? Neither can a salt spring produce fresh water.

— (James 3:6-12 NIV)

Did you know this was in the Bible? This is an eye- opening, animated description of the tongue.

This little member has the ability to bless or curse, and set the course of one's life. It's like a rudder on a ship, steering you into financial abundance or ruin. James also puts the tongue in the same class as an animal which needs to be tamed.

The person who has an untamed tongue will say they believe God is their source. Then, they say they can't tithe or give because they have too many bills to pay. They come to the altar to tell God how good He is and before they get home from church on Sunday they declare they have no idea how to make ends meet! That's not you is it ? What's the truth? Who can tame this crazy thing? As of yet, no man has been able to tame the tongue. But I have some more good news; your Father has even made provision for your crazy tongue.

Why So Much Talk About The Tongue?

Why is there so much talk about the tongue? As you have seen, the tongue is a very unruly member of the body if it's left to itself. We have to go back to the beginning to see why the tongue is so important. Let's look at a text from the book of Genesis for a moment.

And God said, Let there be light: and there was light. And God saw the light, that it was good: and God divided the light from the darkness. And God called the light Day, and the darkness he called Night. And the evening and the morning were the first day. And God said, Let there be a firmament in the midst of the waters, and let it divide the waters from the waters.

— (Genesis 1:3-6 KJV)

As we continue to read through Genesis, this same pattern continues from verse three through verse twenty-six, but notice how this creative discourse ends in verse thirty-one.

And God saw everything that he had made, and, behold, it was very good. And the evening and the morning were the sixth day.

— (Genesis 1:31 KJV)

God saw everything He made. Well, when did He actually make anything? He made everything when He spoke words. God spoke good words- creative words, and when He was done He said it was very good. Can you say the same thing about the words you have spoken over your finances? When you are done with your creative process do you say, "This is very good"? What you have been saying about your finances has shown up. You and I are created in the image and likeness of our Father. We are a representation of the Godhead, (Father, Son, and Holy Spirit), with the same creative ability in our mouth. We are literally a "speaking spirit" with creative power in our mouth just like our Father!

One day I was meditating on a verse of Scripture in Psalms concerning the words of my mouth.

May the words of my mouth and this meditation of my heart be pleasing and acceptable in your sight, Lord, my Rock and my Redeemer.

— (Psalm 19:14 NIV)

As I was reading this, the Holy Spirit told me to look at the phrase, "words of my mouth" and "pleasing in your sight". It was like someone turned on a light bulb. I realized God sees my words as a finished product. He gets a picture of what I create with my tongue. If you think this sounds far-fetched, consider this: We have already established that God saw what He spoke. But let me put a little twist on this: He also spoke what He saw (in Himself). What was in Him, was released by the power of His words. In essence, when He released His words it was already created, even before it was seen! Your words have that much power too!

When you speak you see in pictures, not in words. If I say the word car, you will immediately see a car. You don't see c-a-r. Do you? You speak what you see (internally) and see what you speak. Wrap your mind around this concept and don't let it go. You are creating your financial world every time you open your mouth. When you say, " I can't afford that", you create an image of lack in your life and before God. Since our God is a God of abundance, overflow and more than enough, I am convinced words like this aren't pleasing in His sight.

The Bible says in **Matthew 12:36** we will give an account for every idle- non productive, worthless word we speak. God says in **Luke 21:33**, heaven and earth will pass away before His Word will pass away. I get the feeling words are really important to God. It appears words hang around a long time, if we have to give an account to God for them! Before you open your mouth concerning your finances you better ask yourself a few questions, " Is what I'm about to say what I really want? Is it pleasing before the Father? Will my words create the financial image and likeness my Father has designed for me or will they be words which interrupt or hinder His financial flow in my life"?

Can you see why there is so much talk about the tongue? Your tongue will make or break your financial future. I have always said, "the lack or abundance of money starts in your mouth"! After reading this chapter I trust you are now armed with life changing revelation. From this day forward I pray you will be keenly aware of the words you permit to escape from your lips.

What Are You Saying About Yourself?

Stop putting yourself down today! It doesn't matter how you got into the financial fix you are in. You might have made some foolish financial decisions, but that's ok. What matters from this point on is what you decide to do with your tongue now that you know what an important role it plays in your financial well-being. Today you have the power to turn the tables on your tongue. You can use your tongue like a pen and write out a new financial future.

My heart is stirred by a noble theme as I recite my verses for the king; my tongue is the pen of a skillful writer.
— (Psalm 45:1 NIV)

Begin to declare Word of God in the area of finances and skillfully design the financial future you have always dreamed of. As an ambassador of Christ you have authority to you decree and declare things.

Thou shalt also decree a thing, and it shall be established unto thee: and the light shall shine upon thy ways.

— (Job 22:28- KJV)

You're the one to make financial declaration. When you do, you will be established, firm and immoveable. You're the only one who can tame the tongue with the Word of God. Don't pray and ask God to help you with your tongue. He has already helped you when He gave you a book called the Bible, loaded with living words in it. Use it. Begin by putting the living Word of God in your mouth and talk to your finances for a change instead of allowing them to talk to you. Turn the tables on your tongue and use it for your benefit. When you make your declaration, light will shine on your path. When you make up your "mouth" to declare the Word of God over your financial mess, then the Holy Spirit will shine the light of His glory on your path so you can break out of poverty into financial abundance. Hallelujah! What powerful revelation.

Bridge The Tongue And Heart together

Here's a final word on the tongue. We have spent a great deal of time dealing with this area and rightly so; it will set the course of your life. I purposely didn't start this book with Biblical financial principles because that's the obvious starting point. You probably already know most of the principles we are going to talk about, but principles alone won't work. This is why we covered the other critical areas first. I used to believe if I tithed and gave offerings money had to show up. This is very far from the truth if the previous chapters are left undone. I tithed and gave for almost ten years before I finally understood, by revelation of the Holy Spirit, that my heart and tongue needed to be in agreement with my actions in order to see the financial blessings the Bible speaks of. Let me restate what we have learned in another way before we move on to the financial principles.

Imagine for a moment the mouth and heart are hooked up together by a string. When the mouth opens and speaks it pulls on the door of the heart and overflow occurs. When the flap called the mouth is opened, it will reveal what is in the heart. Whatever the mouth speaks will manifest IF you believe it in your heart.

For verily I say unto you, That whosoever shall <u>say</u> unto this mountain, Be thou removed, and be thou cast into the sea; and shall not doubt in his heart, but shall believe that those things which he <u>saith</u> shall come to pass; he shall have whatsoever he <u>saith</u>. Therefore I say unto you,

What things soever ye desire, when ye pray, believe that ye receive them, and ye shall have them.

— (Mark 11:23-24 KJV).

There are some folks reading right now who are experiencing a disconnect or short between the heart and the tongue. They're saying all of the right stuff, but the heart string is not attached so there is no manifestation. The Bible refers to this state as a sinful and unbelieving heart- **Hebrews 3:12**.

Numbers 32:23 says our sins will find us out. May I add, your faith will also find you out! If you are truly in faith, the Word will become a living reality in your life. Remember this: In order for any of the Biblical principles to work effectively, the heart and mouth must be in agreement with your actions and the Word of God. You can't think one thing about your finances and speak another or vice versa. Your faith will find you out so build a bridge between the heart and the tongue.

Chapter 6

Break Down The Wall of Financial Containment

So you ask " How do I break down the walls of financial containment?" How do I break out of this financial rut and get off the hamster wheel of lack?" The first financial principle we will apply to break down the walls of financial containment is the tithe. Yes, I said the tithe. For some in the body of Christ, it's become a dirty five letter word. Many pastors are afraid to teach the people the truth concerning the tithe. They leave a basket at the back door or apologize to the people for having to receive it. After reading this chapter I guarantee you will have a whole new mindset about the tithe.

There was a pastor I knew who asked the people in his church to give $20 each week to make sure the church bills were paid. He felt if he had them give in this way, he wouldn't have to "pressure" the people to give. I can't find this type of instruction anywhere in my Bible. When a man or woman of God compromises the Word to please the people, disaster is the only logical outcome. Later there was another area of compromise in his teaching in the area of homosexuality. A few months later he passed away. I am not saying this to be judgmental, but I do believe this happened because of these key areas where he began to lead God's people astray. My point is this: if you teach the Gospel then stay committed to teach just the Gospel. Don't teach what's comfortable for you or the people. Just teach the Word and let God do the rest.

Another tactic used in the church is the practice of collecting church dues. When did the church become a country club? Somebody forgot to tell me! You see, we've been trying to escape this command since Malachi chapter three was written and still can't figure out why we are broke, busted and disgusted. I was horrified to find out how many sinners tithe, in contrast to so called "believers" who don't believe in tithing!

I could mention some very prominent people in the secular world who tithe and you would be shocked too . They are working the very same Biblical principles our Father gave us and they are prospering. What an indictment against the body of Christ! Jesus spoke in a parable about this in **Luke 16**.

"The master commended the dishonest manager because he had acted shrewdly. <u>For the people of this world are more shrewd in dealing with their own kind than are the people of the light.</u>

— (Luke 16:8 NIV)

The first key to breaking down the wall of financial containment is to renew your mind concerning the tithe. Let's explore this subject further.

The Great Exchange

If I told you I can show you how returning one dime from every dollar could change your life would you be interested in listening? Let's find out how this exchange can begin to set the stage for an outpouring of the blessing from the Father.

One of the main chapters quoted on Sunday morning during offering time in churches all across the nation is a few verses from Malachi chapter three; You know the part about the windows of heaven being opened, being cursed with a curse and so on. In order to get the full revelation of the tithe, let's go back to Genesis and find out how it was introduced and what the intended purpose was. We are going back to the beginning because the first thing our Christian counterparts will mention when disputing the tithe is, "tithing was under the Law and we are under grace". People love to pull out the grace card when it's convenient for them. Don't they? We will handle this misconception right away.

Everything we do in life involves some sort of exchange. When we go to the grocery store we exchange cash for food. When we breathe we make an exchange of carbon dioxide for oxygen . When we got saved we exchanged our sin for His righteousness. Now it's strange when it comes to the financial arena, we believe we just pray and money will appear in the mailbox. Prayer is not the designated seed of exchange for the blessing of the tithe. Our father Abraham (in the text below he is called Abram) set the example for us on how to make the great exchange.

This is the first time in Scripture we see the mention of the word tithe. I have heard some people reference Cain and

Abel's offering as the tithe, but this offering refers to what is called the first fruit offering. If you conduct a search in your concordance you will see the tithe and first fruit offerings are referred separately and are not the same thing. Studying this topic alone is another book in itself . For now, let's concentrate on the tithe. **Genesis 14:17-23** is in fact the very first time the word tithe is mentioned in Scripture.

After Abram returned from defeating Kedorlaomer and the kings allied with him, the king of Sodom came out to meet him in the Valley of Shaveh (that is, the King's Valley). Then Melchizedek king of Salem brought out bread and wine. He was priest of God Most High, and he blessed Abram, saying, "Blessed be Abram by God Most High, Creator of heaven and earth. And praise be to God Most High, who delivered your enemies into your hand." Then Abram gave him a tenth of everything. The king of Sodom said to Abram, "Give me the people and keep the goods for yourself." But Abram said to the king of Sodom, "With raised hand I have sworn an oath to the Lord, God Most High, Creator of heaven and earth, that I will accept nothing belonging to you, not even a thread or the strap of a sandal, so that you will never be able to say, 'I made Abram rich.'

— (Genesis 14:17-23 NIV)

Melchizedek was king and High Priest of that day. He is also a "type of " Christ, who is our High Priest. Try to imagine for a moment this scenario as it unfolds. Abram met Melchizedek in the Valley of Shaveh after a fierce battle. Melchizedek brought out bread and wine- symbolic of a covenant being made. Melchizedek pronounces "the blessing" over Abram and he makes the exchange by giving him a tithe of everything. I didn't notice any mention about the Law in this text or in any of the preceding chapters leading up to this exchange because tithing has absolutely nothing to do with the Law. It was given in exchange for the blessing. Notice the statement Abram made to the King of Sodom:

With raised hand I have sworn an oath to the Lord, God Most High, Creator of heaven and earth, that I will accept nothing belonging to you, not even a thread or the strap of a sandal, so that you will never be able to say, 'I made Abram rich.

When did he make the oath? When Abram and Melchizedek, the High Priest made the covenant when they exchanged bread and wine. Abram raised his hand and made an oath before the Most High God, Creator of heaven and earth. Abram made it known that El Elyon, the Most High God was his source and no one else could take His place or take credit for making him rich If Abram expected to be rich as a result of making the exchange what should you expect? Abram knew the exchange of the tithe for the blessing was the catalyst to great wealth and abundance in every area. It's time for us to come to the same conclusion.

The "great exchange" is the **tithe for the blessing**. It's the one dime per dollar we have been wrestling with and debating over for years. It's a critical key to breaking down the wall of financial containment. As a matter of fact it's the only way to break out of poverty into financial abundance.

Recognize Your Source

I especially love how Abram refers to God as " Lord, God Most High, Creator of heaven and earth". He saw God as his divine source of everything. The Most High God was able to sustain him and provide everything he needed, wanted and desired because Abram made the great exchange. The world system had nothing to offer him. The world system has nothing compared to our God! Knowing who He is and the revelation you have gained concerning the purpose of the tithe should remove all barriers when it comes to trusting your Father with your financial future.

When the Jews became indignant with Jesus they said: **"Abraham is our father," they answered. "If you were**

Abraham's children," said Jesus, "then you would do what Abraham did.

— (John 8:39 NIV)

If the blessing of Abraham (in this case Abram) is ours then we better start doing what our forefather did. For one thing, he was a tither. He wasn't afraid or ashamed to declare the Most High God as his source. Not only did he declare it, but he showed proof. His tithe was the **evidence** of his belief; It proved his faith. My Bible says faith without works is dead.

In the same way, faith by itself, if it is not accompanied by action, is dead.

— (James 2:17 NIV)

Don't tell me you have faith to break down the wall of financial containment if you don't exercise your faith with the "work" of the tithe. It's the action which completes your faith. Returning the tithe is the only evidence the Father has of your faith. There is no way you will break down the wall of financial containment if you don't recognize God as your source of everything.

Before I close let me mention a very important fact about the tithe. The tithe does not belong to you, it belongs to God. Personally, I always thought stealing from God was a pretty foolish thing to do. After all, He is God! If you really believe He is who He says He is, you may want to think twice before you pick His pocket. Here are two witnesses to support this truth:

And all the tithe of the land, whether of the seed of the land, or of the fruit of the tree, is the Lord's: it is holy unto the Lord.

— (Leviticus 27:30 KJV)

Will a man rob God? Yet ye have robbed me. But ye say, Wherein have we robbed thee? In tithes and offerings.

— (Malachi 3:8 KJV)

I think back about fourteen years ago when my son was about one and a half years old. I was doing a little work from home which didn't pay much at all. One time, I knew if I tithed, I wasn't going to have any money left over. So, I talked to God and told Him I needed the tithe money to take care of my household. A day or so later, after I stole the money from God, my son came walking down the hall in our apartment, fell down and twisted his ankle. Guess who had to spend money to take him to the doctor and get what he needed to nurse his ankle? Yes, yours truly. I went to God so upset and asked Him why this happened. I will never forget that day as I stood at the sink doing dishes. The Holy Spirit spoke loud and clear in my spirit and said "the devourer did exactly what he was supposed to do". Malachi chapter three flooded my mind and I repented. I promised God I would never steal the tithe again. I was now a believer in what was waiting for me if I stole from my Father again. I was convinced the devourer would be waiting on the other side of my disobedience. That day I decided to trust God and let Him take care of me the way He wanted to. He has never let me down.

How the Father longs for us to trust Him like Abram did. We trust our boss and the government which is flat broke, more than we trust the Most High God, Creator of heaven and the earth! This must be so grievous to the Holy Spirit. Do you really want to break out of poverty into financial abundance? Recognize God as your source. Do what your Father Abram did and make the great exchange.

The Exchange Is The Same Today

The same exchange Abram made is still available for you today. Jesus is now the High Priest who receives our tithes, but we still return it through men. The account we just read in Genesis is mentioned again in Hebrews chapter seven.

This Melchizedek was king of Salem and priest of God Most High. He met Abraham returning from the defeat of the kings and blessed him, and Abraham gave him a tenth of everything. First, the name Melchizedek means "king of righteousness"; then also, "king of Salem" means "king of peace." Without father or mother, without genealogy, without beginning of days or end of life, resembling the Son of God, he remains a priest forever. Just think how great he was: Even the patriarch Abraham gave him a tenth of the plunder! Now the law requires the descendants of Levi who become priests to collect a tenth from the people—that is, from their fellow Israelites— even though they also are descended from Abraham. This man, however, did not trace his descent from Levi, yet he collected a tenth from Abraham and blessed him who had the promises. And without doubt the lesser is blessed by the greater. In the one case, the tenth is collected by people who die; but in the other case, by him who is declared to be living.

— (Hebrews 7:1-8 NIV)

It would be well worth your time to read this chapter in its entirety. It's very easy to glance past the sentence below if you are not careful.

"In the one case, the <u>tenth</u> is collected by people who die; but in the other case, <u>by him who is declared to be living".</u>

At one time the tithe was collected by people who die but now through Him who is declared to be living. Jesus receives the tithe and exchanges it for the blessing. Someone is reading this right now and you are utterly speechless, shocked and amazed to see this reference of the tithe in the New Testament! Let me shock you a little more. Jesus also mentioned the tithe in **Luke 11:42.**

"Woe to you Pharisees, because you give God a tenth of your mint, rue and all other kinds of garden herbs, but you neglect justice and the love of God. You should have practiced the latter without leaving the former undone.

— (Luke 11:42 NIV)

Jesus said yes, you give your tenth but you have forgotten about love and justice. He didn't say, "Didn't you guys know the tithe is under the law? Didn't you know we stopped that practice back in the Old Testament?" Jesus let us know, the exchange- the tithe for the blessing is still just as valid today as it was when Abram walked this earth. How can you dispute the words of your Lord and Savior? Though the characters are different now, the tithe is still for today. Tithing is not an option it is a command. If you refuse to comply, you will never break down the wall of financial containment.

Chapter 7

The Storehouse And
The Windows

Over the next few chapters, we'll look at the blessing from many angles. For now, I really want to spend time analyzing Malachi chapter three in relation to the blessing which accompanies the tithe. I mentioned earlier many people who receive the tithe and offering on Sunday quote this text but usually use it as a means to inflict fear into people. The "cursed with a curse" portion of the text is usually overly emphasized. I don't deny the fact that a person puts him or herself and their household under the curse of poverty when they rob God, but this alone can't be our motivation for obeying God. For the most part, what's lacking during offering time is an impartation of the revelation of the blessing the Father said He would pour out upon us. As you read this chapter and see the heart of your Father concerning the tithe, I am confident you will no longer struggle in this area from this day forth if you are having difficulty with this command/principle.

A few years ago I had a conversation with my mother and I told her " I have never seen any windows open enough to experience a blessing I didn't have room enough to receive." In my limited mind, I thought God filled my mailbox with money when I returned the tithe. But once I became tired of not experiencing what I thought the intent of this promise was, I began to do some very in depth study. Ignorance is not bliss. I don't know who came up with that saying, but I would love to tell them a thing or too! If we're not experiencing the manifestation of the promises in Scripture, it's our job to search out the truth and gain knowledge and understanding. Timothy admonishes us to rightly divide the word of truth. When we do this we will not be ashamed of the Word not working in our lives nor will we continue to bring an aspect of shame on the body of Christ for failing to manifest the certain promises of God.

Study to shew thyself approved unto God, a workman that needeth not to be ashamed, rightly dividing the word of truth.

— (2 Timothy 2:15 KJV)

The Bible says in **Hoses 4:6**

My people are destroyed for lack of knowledge: because thou hast rejected knowledge, I will also reject thee, that thou shalt be no priest to me: seeing thou hast forgotten the law of thy God, I will also forget thy children.

— (Hosea 4:6 KJV)

When this text is quoted most people stop at the first portion of it. It goes on to say "thou has rejected knowledge". The lack of knowledge really isn't the problem because there is plenty available. Our society is on the cutting edge of technology in every area. We have more spiritual insight and education than they ever had in the Old Testament, yet we are not manifesting the Word as our forefathers did. So what seems to be the problem with the lack of financial manifestation across the board in the body of Christ? On the contrary, the knowledge is available and being taught, **but it's being rejected**. We have a habit of picking and choosing what we want to believe is the truth. Since we have chosen to reject God's knowledge, He said He would reject us as His priests and forget our children. This is a sobering text! The priest sets the spiritual climate of the earth. They bring the culture of the kingdom of God into earth as His ambassadors. If I state this more plainly; you pretty much lose your job as priest and God said He will forget your children as well. This gives new insight into what we term as "generational curses". Could it be the rejection of knowledge which has opened the door for the curse to invade our families and finances?

As we embark on this journey to uncover the blessing found in Malachi chapter three concerning the tithe, we will break down this text so you will have a clearer picture and more firm grasp on the Father's intent concerning the tithe.

So God said He would open the windows of heaven and pour out a blessing you would not have room enough to receive. It sounds good but what does it mean? Once when my pastor was meditating on the Word, the Holy Spirit asked him "What does it look like?" What does it look like when the blessing is poured out? Let's continue to take this one step at a time and we will find out.

Where Is The Storehouse?

Bring ye all the tithes into the storehouse, that there may be meat in mine house, and prove me now herewith, saith the Lord of hosts, if I will not open you the windows of heaven, and pour you out a blessing, that there shall not be room enough to receive it.

— (Malachi 3:10 KJV)

The storehouse is the place where you are "fed" the Word of God. If you are confined to your home and watch a particular ministry on T.V., then send them your tithe. If you are a pastor then send your tithe outside of your church to a man of God who feeds you. Every pastor should have someone who can teach them. The Father always has a fresh word for whosoever has ears to hear. If you attend a church regularly, then this is the place you are fed and your tithe should be deposited there. I have heard some people say they don't tithe at the church they attend because they're not learning or growing. Well, what are you doing there? Find a local church which is teaching the Word!

The tithe shouldn't be given to the poor or split between your favorite ministries. This verse does not say storehouses-plural. There should be a certain place where your tithe is returned. There should be a "certain brook" you have been called to be fed and to be a blessing. You can send other ministries an offering or give to the poor as led by the Holy Spirit (we will cover the offering in a later chapter), but the tithe goes to the storehouse.

If I permit you to hold something for me and give you instructions on how to handle it, what do you think I would expect from you? I expect you to carry out my instructions with whatever I have entrusted to you. The same principle applies to the tithe. Since the tithe is not yours, you should follow the instructions of the One who entrusted it to you. The Bible is one of the least confusing books I have ever read. I think we complicate it with all of our "soulish" insight. The tithe goes to your storehouse.

The Significance Of The "Windows of Heaven"

If you go back and study the word windows, you will find out the windows of heaven mentioned in Malachi chapter three are the same windows which were opened on the earth during the flood of Noah's day.

In the six hundredth year of Noah's life, in the second month, the seventeenth day of the month, the same day were all the fountains of the great deep broken up, and the windows of heaven were opened.

— (Genesis 7:11 KJV)

The Hebrew word for windows is **"arubbah".** It is derived from the word Arab which means to ambush or lie in wait. **Arubbah** means a sluice or water channel in which the water flow is controlled by a gate to hold it back. Do you remember how much rain came through the windows of heaven during the flood of Noah's day? It was enough to cover the entire earth! Every living creature which wasn't in the ark was completely covered and died. This is the same floodgate of blessing the Father said He has opened upon you and your household when you return the tithe to the storehouse.

The gate is already opened to flood your financial situation with abundance, overflow and increase!

Going back to the word Arab, which Arubbah is derived from, think of this: when you return the tithe from this day forward, get a picture of the Father "violently" ambushing you with the blessing flow to a point where you are literally trying to catch your breath to keep your head above the water. See Him overtaking you with the blessing when you return the tithe to the storehouse. This sounds awesome right? So what is the blessing He's pouring out, money, right? You'll find out the truth very shortly.

Chapter 8

The Reality Of
The Blessing

I know I'm not alone, but I was ignorant of the blessing which was released from tithing for a long long time. I thought the blessing was money and things. That's what I was looking for. I was financially blessed but not a "windows of heaven blessing", or so I thought. It was more like a hit and miss for me. Sometimes it worked better than other times.

The word blessing in the Hebrew is **" berakah"**, which means benediction- to speak over; to invoke prosperity- to include health, happiness, wellness, favor and goodness in every area of your life. We have to go back to Genesis to get the first mention and intent of the blessing. Adam and Eve were the first recipients of the blessing.

God blessed them and said to them, "Be fruitful and increase in number; fill the earth and subdue it. Rule over the fish in the sea and the birds in the sky and over every living creature that moves on the ground."

— (Genesis 1:28 NIV)

What did God do to them to bless them? How did He bless them? He **spoke words over them**. Hang on to this for a moment and we will pull things together at the end of this chapter.

For another witness, let's look at Genesis twenty-seven when Jacob deceived Isaac and stole the blessing from Esau. After Isaac and Esau realized what Jacob had done look at their response. Please go back and read the full account on your own.

And Isaac his father said unto him, Who art thou? And he said, I am thy son, thy firstborn Esau. And Isaac trembled very exceedingly, and said, Who? where is he that hath taken venison, and brought it me, and I have eaten of all before thou camest, and have blessed him? yea, and he shall be blessed. And when Esau heard the words of his father, he cried with a great and exceeding bitter cry, and said unto his father, Bless me, even me also, O my father.

And he said, Thy brother came with subtilty, and hath taken away thy blessing.

— (Genesis 27:32-35 KJV)

Looking at the text above, why do you suppose Isaac **"trembled very exceedingly"**? He was literally terrified when he realized he had been deceived to release the blessing upon an unintended receiver. Why? Because the blessing is real! When it's spoken over a person he/she will literally be endowed with every word spoken over their life. The blessing is as real as any tangible thing in this earth- even more so! This goes back again to the words of our mouth. What you speak over yourself and your children will definitely manifest. You can invoke the benediction, or you can invoke a curse. Isaac was fearful because this empowerment to prosper had been stolen from his firstborn son. He knew when the blessing was conferred upon an individual, they would be blessed indeed and nothing could stop it from being fulfilled. Follow the life of Abraham, Jacob or Isaac through to the end and you will find out they were" blessed indeed". The blessing was on their lives and the manifestation couldn't be denied. The same benediction God spoke over Adam and Eve and your forefathers, has been spoken over you. This same blessing rested on Jesus. Did you ever read of Jesus being in want or need of anything? No! Because the Father spoke a blessing over Him, "This is my son in whom I am well pleased". He's said the same thing about you. You are an heir of God and joint heir with Christ Jesus (Romans 8:17), so it would go without saying, you have access to the same blessing as you obey the Father.

You Can't Curse
What God Has blessed

In Numbers chapter twenty-two, Balak, The king of the Moabites sent his servants to summon Balaam to place a curse upon the Israelites. God warned Balaam in a nice way on the first two occasions not to go with the men to curse his people. When Balaam asked a third time God told him to go, but the Lord's anger burned against him because he kept coming to God to curse the Israelites even though God told him not to go with the men. Once Balaam arrived to meet Balak, he took him to three different locations to curse the Israelites, but each time he could only speak the words God put in his mouth - words of blessing. If you follow this charade through to Numbers chapter twenty-four, here is what occurs on his last attempt to speak a curse over God's people:

the prophecy of one who hears the words of God, who sees a vision from the Almighty, who falls prostrate, and whose eyes are opened: "How beautiful are your tents,

Jacob, your dwelling places, Israel! "Like valleys they spread out, like gardens beside a river, like aloes planted by the Lord, like cedars beside the waters. Water will flow from their buckets; their seed will have abundant water. "Their king will be greater than Agag; their kingdom will be exalted."God brought them out of Egypt; they have the strength of a wild ox. They devour hostile nations and break their bones in pieces; with their arrows they pierce them. Like a lion they crouch and lie down, like a lioness—who dares to rouse them? "May those who bless you be blessed and those who curse you be cursed!" Then Balak's anger burned against Balaam. He struck his hands together and said to him, "I summoned you to curse my enemies, but you have blessed them these three times. Now leave at once and go home! I said I would reward you handsomely, but the Lord has kept you from being rewarded." Balaam answered Balak, "Did I not tell the messengers you sent me, 'Even if Balak gave me all the silver and gold in his palace, I could not do anything of my own accord, good or bad, to go beyond the command of the Lord—and I must say only what the Lord says'?

— (Numbers 24:4-13 NIV)

My friend, you can't curse what God has blessed. The blessing is so powerful! The blessing is real. It's the key to abundance, overflow, wellness happiness, health, wealth, prosperity and the favor of God in every area of your life!

For the most part this news doesn't excite many people because it's not a tangible thing and it doesn't come out of a microwave or through a drive-thru window. Think about this for a moment, if God has spoken happiness, wellness, favor, wealth and prosperity over your life in the same magnitude as that of the windows of heaven opened during the flood of Noah's time, what do you think your life should look like? He is the same God who said "let there be", and it appeared. He saw everything He spoke. What do you think will happen if you embrace the reality of the blessing? I will let you come to your own conclusion on this thought.

Many times we throw the word blessing around like a Frisbee. When someone asks how we are, we say, "Blessed and highly favored", but a very high percentage of the body of Christ has no clue of the value of the blessing. From this day forward, when you say you are blessed or when you declare the Father has opened the windows of heaven and poured out a blessing you don't have room enough to receive, you now have revelation. You know He has spoken empowering words over your life to prosper you in every way. For the record, He didn't leave out your money! That was included too. Otherwise, He wouldn't have told you to be blessed to be a blessing until all ends of the earth are blessed. That would be a pretty tough bill to fill without money.

I adjure you in the matchless name of the Lord Jesus Christ to receive by faith your blessing package. Your life will never be the same. No one can stop you when you realize you have already been set up for a "bless up" by the Father. But, it doesn't do you any good to know about the blessing if you don't know how to apply it to your life. This would rank in line with quoting Scriptures without any manifestation; and we both know there's a whole lot of that going on and it doesn't work.

So What Do I Do With The Blessing?

You might be saying "Ok, I understand and believe what you are saying about the blessing, but what do I do with words? I need to pay my mortgage and my kids need money for college. How do I turn words into tangible things?" First of all, you have to receive them by faith and be in agreement with what the Father says about you in the area of finances. We talked about the importance of words a few chapters ago. The blessing is ineffective if you aren't going to be in agreement with what He has already said concerning your financial status. Let me pause right here and interject to the religious folks; the blessing is not just about financial abundance, it covers every single area of your life.

Can two walk together, except they are agree?
— (Amos 3:3 KJV)

You can't walk in the blessing unless you're in agreement with the giver of the blessing. The Greek definition for saying the same thing is **homologia** from the word **homologeo** which means to say the same thing as another; to declare; to confess; to profess.

We see it used here in Hebrews.

Let us hold unswervingly to the hope we <u>profess</u>, for he who promised is faithful.
— (Hebrews 10:23 NIV

You activate the blessing by first returning the tithe and **saying the same thing** the Father says about you. You see how these chapters are building upon each other? Declare and confess the same thing the Father says in order to activate the blessing in your life. If you're confessing your present circumstances, you have stepped out from under the umbrella of the blessing. You don't walk by sight do you?

Not if you're a Christian. You walk by faith. Speaking the blessing is the way your Father introduced health, wellness, favor, wholeness and prosperity into your life. It's the only way for you to activate and walk in it.

This is why you need to study and read the Word daily. If your words are going to agree with God's words, it might do you some good to know what He says about you and your financial abundance. If your current financial status doesn't look like the Word, then there has been a breakdown in the covenant on your part, not His.

Get your concordance out and start looking up Scriptures on abundance and the blessing. You can also save some time and purchase our **"Seeds of Prosperity CD"** and booklet which is loaded with Scripture in this area. Get your blessing flow started today. Speak what He speaks.

Stay with me, we are still putting the pieces together. You will have full clarity on what to do with the blessing before this chapter is over. Tithing and speaking the blessing are the first two principles to activate it.

Your Position In The Blessing

In Proverbs 10:22, the Bible says

the blessing of the Lord maketh rich and he adds no sorrow with it.

The word sorrow in the Hebrew means to toil. The blessing takes the place of toiling. This cursed state entered the scene when Adam listened to his wife Eve and disobeyed God.

To Adam he said, "Because you listened to your wife and ate fruit from the tree about which I commanded you, 'You must not eat from it,' "Cursed is the ground because of you; through painful toil you will eat food from it all the days of your life. It will produce thorns and thistles for you, and you will eat the plants of the field. By the sweat of your brow you will eat your food until you return to the ground, since from it you were taken; for dust you are and to dust you will return."

— (Genesis 3:17-19 NIV)

Well what was Adam doing before he began to work by the sweat of the brow? He tended the garden with the **words of his mouth.** He spoke things into existence just like his Father did. You see, toiling should not be and never was the position for a child of God to be in; it's the position of fallen unredeemed man. The "sweat of the brow" is how those under the world system make a living. It's the state which those outside of the blessing find themselves in. They are constantly trying to make provision for themselves through working long hours, overtime, double time and at least two jobs. What's unfortunate about this is many believers have no idea they have shifted positions in the spiritual realm, when they received Christ as their Lord and are still operating under the curse in the area of finances. We have taken our position as saved and many have now accepted their position of healing, but we are still in a fight of our lives to get the body of Christ to take their position in the blessing – especially when it comes to our money.

If you accept the blessing by faith and activate it according to what we have learned so far, you move from the position of fallen man- toiling, back to your original position of abundance. This place of abundance is the Garden of Eden. It is the spot of the presence of God. As a body, we desperately need our financial situation to resemble a spot of the presence of God.

Let me close this section by saying this: When God blessed Adam and Eve He wanted them to take the garden atmosphere beyond the garden. The earth was not like the garden. This is why the Father told them to subdue the earth.

And God blessed them, and God said unto them, Be fruitful, and multiply, and replenish the earth, and subdue it: and have dominion over the fish of the sea, and over the fowl of the air, and over every living thing that moveth upon the earth.

— (Genesis 1:28)

It looks like we have been getting subdued by the earth but it's time to turn the tables now that you are in your position of blessing.

Look For The Instruction and Seize The Opportunities

Here's what you have been waiting for. What I am about to say in this section will change your financial status if you have ears to hear! Now I can reveal why I never saw the windows of heaven open up for me and pour out a "blessing" I did not have room enough to receive, even though it was happening all around me. I had no idea, whenever I returned my tithe and gave my offering (we'll get to the offering), instruction, opportunities and ideas always followed.

The blessing is manifested in your life through receiving instruction, opportunities and ideas from the Holy Spirit. Health, wellness, favor and prosperity can be seen.

If you get a job you're really not qualified for, that's the manifestation of the favor of God. Your income has now increased. If you purchase a car at a dealership the Holy Spirit sends you to and it's deeply discounted "for no apparent reason", or so they think, you know it's a manifestation of the blessing in your life. I could go on and on, but I hope you picked up on a key element concerning the instruction, ideas and opportunities. You have to be sensitive to and obey the voice of the Holy Spirit.

Thus saith the Lord, thy Redeemer, the Holy One of Israel; I am the Lord thy God which teacheth thee to profit, which leadeth thee by the way that thou shouldest go.

— (Isaiah 48:17 KJV)

Somebody is saying " I knew there was a catch!" The Holy Spirit is the only person who can give you instruction and reveal the ideas and opportunities to you. Because I didn't know how the blessing manifested ten years ago, I just sat around waiting on God. This is why we miss the "windows of heaven blessing". It's waiting at every turn to ambush us but we keep waiting on God to deliver the finished product. We want our blessing like we get our food out of the microwave in three minutes or less. My friend, you are the only one who can reap your harvest. Listen for the instruction. Look for the opportunity or idea and go for it!

Do you remember when Moses was standing at the Red Sea in Exodus? He told the Israelites **God** was going to deliver them, to just wait and see what **God** was going to do. Let's look at this account.

Moses answered the people, "Do not be afraid. Stand firm and you will see the deliverance the Lord will bring you today. The Egyptians you see today you will never see again. The Lord will fight for you; you need only to be still." Then the Lord said to Moses, "Why are you crying out to me? Tell the Israelites to move on. Raise your staff and stretch out your hand over the sea to divide the water so that the Israelites can go through the sea on dry ground.

— (Exodus 14:13-16 NIV)

What had to happen in order for deliverance to take place? An instruction had to be given and obeyed. God asked

Moses "Why are you crying out to me"? God gave Moses instruction to stretch out his rod and his obedience caused the deliverance of a nation. What do you think would have happened to the Israelites if Moses kept talking about what God was going to do; just waiting on the Lord? I can tell you that would have been the end of that story and the rest of the Bible! This is definitely a picture of what a "windows of heaven" blessing looks like.

We do the same thing today as Moses did. We talk about how good God is; how He is going to come through for us and deliver us. This is true, but I believe He is asking the body of Christ the same question today. "Why are you crying out to Me for rent, gas and food money?" Instead we should be asking for instruction or ideas and looking for opportunities.

If you're a tither and giver and still not walking in the blessing, I venture to say you are missing the instruction, ideas and opportunities He's presenting to you. Something is definitely wrong and it's not on God's part. Every time you tithe and give, an instruction, opportunity or idea will **ALWAYS** follow. You must be ready to hear and obey. Don't live your life sitting around waiting for the mailman to bring you a breakthrough. Your breakthrough has already been released by way of ideas, opportunities and instruction from the Holy Spirit- the Teacher of profit. It's up to you to yield your ear to the Him so He can lead you. When you obey His voice, you'll realize the opportunity, idea or instruction is the gateway to your harvest.

Chapter 9

Say Good-Bye To
The Devourer

Have you ever felt like you had a purse with holes in it? I have. I tithed for years and still couldn't get ahead. I would advance financially but something always happened to eat up my return. I went from one financial dilemma to another. One evening I went to the Lord and asked Him why this was happening to me. I stated my case as a tither and reminded Him of His promises in Malachi chapter three. The Holy Spirit told me to go get my Bible and turn to Malachi chapter three. After He told me this I said, " I know what that chapter says!" I am so thankful for God's patience with His "all- knowing" children. When I opened my Bible and began reading, everything looked as usual until I got to verse eight.

Will a man rob God? Yet ye have robbed me. But ye say, Wherein have we robbed thee? In tithes and offerings.

— (Malachi 3:8)

The tail end of this verse caught my attention. Four words stood up off the page as if someone had literally shone a neon light on them **"IN TITHES AND OFFERINGS".** Up until this point I had no clue the tithe and offering were the connection to the covenant of blessing. God said, you rob in me in **tithes and offerings.** I thought I only needed to tithe, but now I saw He expected me to bring an offering as well! You see, we can read and read and still not "see" the truth until the Holy Spirit gives us revelation. I repented right then and there and made up my mind to begin obeying Him right away. Partial obedience is still disobedience, whether we are aware of our disobedience or not. It's our job to search out the Scriptures. We do a lot of things in part and when we don't see the results, we get upset with God. When you put the tithe and offering together, verse eleven is now yours to declare and see manifested in your life.

And I will rebuke the devourer for your sakes, and he shall not destroy the fruits of your ground; neither shall your vine cast her fruit before the time in the field, saith the Lord of hosts.

— (Malachi 3:11 KJV)

The Hebrew word for devourer is **Akal**. It means to eat, consume or burn up. Satan is the devourer. He shows up to eat or destroy the harvest you have coming to you. When you tithe and give your offering, his job is to hinder or delay your harvest to see if you will stand on your covenant rights. When you obey the Word, God comes like a patriot missile to intercept Satan's attack against you. You can't rebuke the devourer by words. You can't pray the devourer out of your life. You can speak in tongues day and night but nothing is going to happen. You have to be a tither and giver to have a case against him. When you practice this kingdom financial principle, God promises to step in and prevent the enemy from destroying your harvest.

What's In A Rebuke?

The word rebuke literally means stop it, that's enough! God will tell Satan, " I have drawn the line and you can't go any farther. This one is under my covenant and you can't touch this". Listen to me carefully; this is not an automatic occurrence. When the devourer shows up you have to be the one to enforce your covenant authority by reminding the Father of His Word. Is God forgetful? No, but you have to declare the Word to give Him the legal right to intervene on your behalf. God will permit what you will permit. You have been given complete dominion and authority in this earth. You are the legal agent here, so it's up to you to call God into your situation by declaring His Word.

When David heard how Goliath taunted the Israelites for forty days, he became incensed that someone would defy the armies of the Living God.

David asked the men standing near him, "What will be done for the man who kills this Philistine and removes this disgrace from Israel? Who is this <u>uncircumcised</u> Philistine that he should defy the armies of the living God?"

— (1 Samuel 17:26 NIV)

Goliath is a picture of what the devourer looks like. He stands waiting to overtake and consume your harvest as you come forth to reap. When we declare our covenant right as a tither and giver, God must show up every time. David recognized he was a man with a covenant and Goliath was not. This is why he referred to him as an "uncircumcised Philistine". David knew his rights. The only thing standing between David and his harvest- the hand of the king's daughter in marriage and exemption from taxes for his family was Goliath!

The one who knows and declares his covenant will always trump the devourer. David showed us how the Father responds when the enemy comes to prevent us from receiving what is rightfully ours. See the Father saying on your behalf, "that's enough, the buck stops here!" The line has been drawn in the sand. He will come in and behead the devourer for your sake. Now if you just stand there like the Israelites did for forty days and let "Goliath" harass you, then there is nothing the Father can do. Satan will eat you alive!

If I showed up on your job on Friday, picked up your pay check after you had worked forty hours, cashed it and had a good old time with your money, I don't think you would take that too lightly. Do you know why? Because you know I have no legal right to take what belongs to you. You'll do whatever is within your legal means to make sure I am prosecuted to the fullest extent of the law. Do you see where I am going with this? You need to have that same tenacity and determination with your financial covenant. What's the point of tithing and giving if you're going to stand by and allow Satan to come in and wreak havoc in your life? You must activate your covenant like David did. David declared his covenant and the Lord fulfilled His Word.

I wonder how many harvests have been abandoned by believers who fled when the devourer showed up, instead of calling on the One who promised to rebuke him. It's time to say good-bye to the devourer. He's had his way in your finances, marriage, physical body and home long enough! You never know where he'll show up but I promise you he will. He is going to see if he can get you to abort your harvest and abandon your covenant. As a tither and a giver you have a right to go before the court of the Most High God and enforce your right for protection. When you do, God will rebuke the devourer. He will prevent him from coming in an eating up your seed or your harvest. Why don't you go ahead and say good-bye to the devourer!

$\mathcal{C}hapter\ 10$

The Kingdom OF God-
A Seed Based System

The kingdom of God is a seed based system. Everything you have learned up to this point will be futile if you don't grasp these last few chapters. What I am about to teach from this point on has the power to eradicate every financial dilemma and produce a financial existence you never imagined possible. Let me make this statement: everything in life comes by way of a seed. You were born from a seed. The words you speak are seed containers that carry out the instructions you give them. The Word of God is a seed. Jesus Himself was a seed. This system of sowing was established back in the beginning and continues on even today.

While the earth remaineth, seedtime and harvest, and cold and heat, and summer and winter, and day and night shall not cease.

— (Genesis 8:22 KJV)

The earth is still here. It still gets hot and cold. We still have summer and winter, so I would venture to say seedtime and harvest are also still in effect. The seed is God's system of multiplying things in the earth. Further, a seed is the **ONLY** way anything in the earth is multiplied or produced. Let's look at some references to validate this premise.

In Mark chapter 4, Jesus began to teach the people how the Word is a seed. When He finished His instruction about the sower and the seed and found himself alone with his disciples, He disclosed the meaning of the parable.

And he began again to teach by the sea side: and there was gathered unto him a great multitude, so that he entered into a ship, and sat in the sea; and the whole multitude was by the sea on the land. And he taught them many things by parables, and said unto them in his doctrine, Hearken; Behold, there went out a sower to sow: And it came to pass, as he sowed, some fell by the way side, and the fowls of the air came and devoured it up. And some fell on stony ground, where it had not much earth; and immediately

it sprang up, because it had no depth of earth: But when the sun was up, it was scorched; and because it had no root, it withered away. And some fell among thorns, and the thorns grew up, and choked it, and it yielded no fruit. And other fell on good ground, and did yield fruit that sprang up and increased; and brought forth, some thirty, and some sixty, and some an hundred.

— (Mark 4:2-8 KJV)

And he said unto them, Unto you it is given to know the mystery of the kingdom of God: but unto them that are without, all these things are done in parables: That seeing they may see, and not perceive; and hearing they may hear, and not understand; lest at any time they should be converted, and their sins should be forgiven them. And he said unto them, Know ye not this parable? and how then will ye know all parables? The sower soweth the word.

— (Mark 4:11-14 KJV)

The only valid and legal place for Word seed to be planted is in the soil of the heart of man. When it's not hindered by the cares of life and finds its way into good soil, it reproduces a harvest "some thirty, and some sixty, and some an hundred."

The Word of God is literally a bag of seed. Whatever you

want to manifest in your life, must first be found in the Word. In order to sow it into your heart effectively and produce corresponding results, you must have full understanding of the Father's intent for the verse. This is what we call revelation. We talked about this when we studied the tithe.

The Word seed is planted in your heart whenever you hear or speak it (**Romans 10:17**). Even if it's not taught or spoken in truth by the deliverer, it's still planted in your heart. This is why I believed money was the root of all evil. Someone planted the Word in my heart but not in accordance with God's truth. I was foolish enough to continue repeating what I heard without checking the Word out for myself. So, be careful who you listen to and always check out the Word for yourself.

Revelation of the Word enables you to declare it with boldness, power and authority. For example, if you planted corn and took care of it like you were supposed to, you wouldn't expect tomatoes to show up because you have revelation of what you planted and what the harvest is supposed to look like. If you sow financial increase seed (from the Word) in your heart with "revelation" and guard it from the enemy and the cares of life, then guess what has to reproduce? Financial abundance! It will happen as long as you are tithing and giving as we discussed previously.

Look at this again, **"And he said unto them, Know ye not this parable? and how then will ye know all parables?"** If I could paraphrase this, Jesus was basically asking them, if you can't understand this parable then how will you be able to understand any other parable in relation to the kingdom, because the kingdom hinges on the seedtime and harvest principle.

There is no other substitute for sowing and reaping, it's the kingdom way. This is totally contrary to the world's way of thinking. The world cares about what you can give them. Their system is a take all you can get system but the kingdom is a sowing and reaping system. If you're not careful, it's pretty easy to brush right past the statement Jesus made in verse **11 "And he said unto them, Unto you it is given to know the mystery of the kingdom of God."**

What is the mystery Jesus was speaking of? It's the mystery of how the kingdom operates as a seed based system. The mystery is: Sowing and reaping, giving and receiving.

In **John 12:20-24** Jesus was preparing the disciples for His death. He compared his body to a natural seed which would go into the ground, but when He was raised up, He would produce many seeds. If you are part of the kingdom, then you are one of the many seeds that was produced because of the death burial and resurrection of Jesus. Here's what I am saying: Jesus was a seed.

Very truly I tell you, unless a kernel of wheat falls to the ground and dies, it remains only a single seed. But if it dies, it produces many seeds.

— (John 12:24 KJV)

Unless a seed is planted in the ground, it will never reproduce. You don't lay apple seed on the counter and come back in a week or so and expect to see an apple tree. You don't put tomato seed in your pocket and expect a tomato vine to grow out of your pocket. The seed must be planted in the ground in order to reproduce.

Haggai had to give the people the same instruction in his day as well.

Is there yet any <u>seed left in the barn</u>? Until now, the vine and the fig tree, the pomegranate and the olive tree have not borne fruit.

— (Haggai 2:19 NIV)

Seed must be planted in good soil. As long as the seed is in any other environment, it will never reproduce. Below is the universal law of sowing and reaping.

Give, and <u>it</u> will be given to you. A good measure, pressed down, shaken together and running over, will be poured into your lap. For with the measure you use, it will be measured to you.

— (Luke 6:38 NIV)

The **"it"** is whatever you decide to give. If you sow evil you will reap evil. If you sow good deeds you will reap them. If you sow discord you will reap discord. One sure thing about any seed sown, it will always return with a greater amount than was originally sown.

Do not be deceived: God cannot be mocked. A man reaps what he sows.

— (Galatians 6:7 NIV)

You can't mock God's system of sowing and reaping. A man can only reap what he's sown. We'll tie this principle together with our finances shortly. One thing I hope you take away from this section is: Sowing and reaping is a kingdom based system of multiplication. There is absolutely no other way to produce abundance without a seed.

The Process Of A Seed

Let's look at another section of **Mark 4,**

And he said, So is the kingdom of God, as if a man should cast seed into the ground;And should sleep, and rise night and day, and the seed should spring and grow up, he knoweth not how. For the earth bringeth forth fruit of herself; first the blade, then the ear, after that the full corn in the ear. But when the fruit is brought forth, immediately he putteth in the sickle, because the harvest is come. And he said, Whereunto shall we liken the kingdom of God? or with what comparison shall we compare it? It is like a grain of mustard seed, which, when it is sown in the earth, is less than all the seeds that be in the earth: But when it is sown, it groweth up, and becometh greater than all herbs, and shooteth out great branches; so that the fowls of the air may lodge under the shadow of it.

— (Mark 4:26-32)

My dad used to plant a garden every year. He would go out there and get the soil ready. He used cow manure and boy did it stink, but this was how he produced beautiful fruits and vegetables every single year. Once he had the soil ready for the seed, he prepared perfectly lined rows in which he would go down and drop his seed in. When he completed each section he covered up the seed with the fertile soil, put a stake up and marked it with the seed package to identify the fruit or vegetable. Like the sower above, my dad would just rise and sleep every night knowing he had a harvest coming. He watered the garden as needed and that was it. I don't recall him ever losing any sleep about the seed. He never panicked about his harvest. My dad didn't know how the soil and seed interacted once he planted it; he just knew he had a harvest coming! He would call my brother and me out to look at the blade as it broke through the ground and brag about how beautiful his cucumbers and tomatoes were going to be. We saw nothing to get excited about, but he saw the "full corn in the ear" even before it showed up. He "saw it before he saw it". Once my dad's garden had ripened, he didn't have someone else come and gather his harvest he did it himself. This concept will prove critical before you can reap your harvest. You have to see it through the eyes of your spirit before you can see it in the natural realm.

As Jesus continued teaching the people, He once again likened the kingdom of God to the same process of sowing as we experience in the natural world. It appears the spiritual and the natural realms run parallel. There is nothing done in the spiritual realm which will not eventually show up in the natural. I can also state it this way: everything in the natural realm found its originating point in the realm of the spirit. The spiritual realm is far more real than the natural.

A person who constantly declares poverty and lack starts a seed process in the spirit realm which will produce a harvest of poverty and lack. When they find themselves in a constant state of "not enough" they're baffled. As Jesus would say, "I tell you the truth," whatever is sown in the spiritual realm goes through the same process as the natural seed and will eventually produce a harvest. Every seed produces after its own kind. You're going to find out shortly this is the very same process your financial seed must undergo.

Chapter 11

The Truth About Money

Money is one of the most talked about and coveted resources in our society. People lose their lives over money every single day. Everything we do centers around money. We pursue higher education for the sole purpose of making more money. People move their families clear across the state for an extra two dollars more per hour. We trade our time in the workplace for money. For many, it has become an object of worship. Jesus spent a lot of time talking about it because He knew the problems we would encounter with it.

When I was growing up I was fearful about having a lot of money because I heard such horrible things about people who had it. Here are some of the things I heard about money as I was growing up: " Rich people don't go to heaven. People who have money got it by hurting someone. If you have a lot of money it's the root of all evil. All you need is just enough to make it." I hate to admit it, but for many years I bought into these lies. It wasn't until I was in my late twenties, I found out the truth about the Scripture below:

For the <u>LOVE</u> of money is a root of all kinds of evil. Some people, eager for money, have wandered from the faith and pierced themselves with many griefs.

— (1 Timothy 6:10 NIV)

About fifteen years ago I got into a conversation with a gentleman who was doing my taxes. He was a mighty man of God who spent a lot of time in the Word studying about finances. He mentioned the misconceptions people have about money. **1 Timothy 6:10** was one of the verses he quoted. When I heard him say "The love of money," my Holy Ghost light bulb came on! I heard this Scripture before but I never heard the full truth about it nor had I ever gone and investigated it on my own. So, I acted like I knew the truth because I was too embarrassed to tell him I was one of those people who thought money was the root of all evil - not the **LOVE** of money. My friend let my former ignorance be a lesson for you. Don't ever take anyone's word when it comes to the Word of God. Look it up for yourself. Always look at the context of the Scripture- read what's before and after it to get a full understanding. This way no one will ever rob you of the truth of the Word. After this encounter, I began my own quest to uncover the truth about money, not by man's standards, but by God's.

After I spoke to the tax man, I was determined to eradicate my false financial blueprint and allow my financial future to be shaped the way God said it was supposed to be. I found out through studying the Word, there is absolutely nothing wrong with money and having lots of it. I found out I could be a blessing if I had some money. I also found out I could enjoy some of the finer things in life. Nobody told me this! The real problem with money arises when we allow money and things to have us!

Jesus addressed the rich young ruler's love of money in **Luke chapter 18,**

A certain ruler asked him, "Good teacher, what must I do to inherit eternal life?" "Why do you call me good?" Jesus answered. "No one is good—except God alone. You know the commandments: 'You shall not commit adultery, you shall not murder, you shall not steal, you shall not give false testimony, honor your father and mother.'" "All these I have kept since I was a boy," he said. When Jesus

heard this, he said to him, "You still lack one thing. Sell everything you have and give to the poor, and you will have treasure in heaven. Then come, follow me." When he heard this, he became very sad, because he was very wealthy. Jesus looked at him and said, "How hard it is for the rich to enter the kingdom of God! Indeed, it is easier for a camel to go through the eye of a needle than for someone who is rich to enter the kingdom of God." Those who heard this asked, "Who then can be saved?" Jesus replied, "What is impossible with man is possible with God." Peter said to him, "We have left all we had to follow you!" "Truly I tell you," Jesus said to them, "no one who has left home or wife or brothers or sisters or parents or children for the sake of the kingdom of God will fail to receive many times as much in this age, and in the age to come eternal life."

— (Luke 18:18-30 NIV)

Jesus knew how to get to the heart of people. Through discernment He knew money and things had a hold on the heart of this young man. You wouldn't believe how many sermons have been preached from this text to convince believers they're supposed to be poor for Jesus- just barely getting by. This rich young ruler didn't understand what Jesus was trying to offer him. He used him as an example to show how hard it is for someone who **trusts in their riches** to enter into the kingdom -God's way of doing things. The rich young ruler would have gotten back everything and more if he had only understood that Jesus was trying to introduce him to the kingdom way of financial increase-sowing and reaping. This Scripture is all about a person who "trusts" in their riches. It's not meant to keep us from aspiring to be wealthy.

Did you also notice the amazement of the disciples when Jesus said it was hard for a rich man to enter the "kingdom of God?" I would venture to guess they were also rich. The disciples were business men. You don't get amazed about something which doesn't describe or affect you. They had a lot of money. In the last verse Jesus said, whatever you give or sow for the kingdom will be multiplied back to you. If being rich was a problem, someone please explain why it would be ok to see it multiplied back to you. The rich young ruler was going to get back even more than he started out with. That would have made him even richer! Do you see the problem with the "rich people can't go to heaven" theory? It's perfectly alright for you to have your stuff and eternal life, if the stuff doesn't have you.

Tell yourself right now, "There's nothing wrong with money and having plenty of it as long as it does not have me!" How in the world are you going to carry the gospel to the ends of the earth without money? There are men and women of God who have various assignments to preach the gospel of the kingdom, who are waiting for your financial support. You might not be called to preach or be a missionary, but you are called to fund this gospel. You are prepared to carry out this mandate now that you know the truth about money.

Chapter 12

Money - Nothin' But A Seed

Want more of it; can't get enough of it; will do anything for it; but it's nothing but a seed. Yes, I am talking about **MONEY**.

For too long we have looked at and held on to money as an end to our means. People hoard and stash it away because they are fearful of not having enough. Many are afraid to give because they see themselves as "giving their money away." This may describe you, but from this point on you will learn money is nothing but a seed. You just need to learn how to skillfully use it.

In the natural an apple seed can only produce an apple tree. A cucumber seed can only produce a vine of cucumbers but money can reproduce into almost anything you want it to be! I like to call it a "universal seed." By this I mean it can take on the form of, adapt to and become a solution to almost every single situation in life. Money answers all things because money is a seed.

A feast is made for laughter, wine makes life merry, and <u>money is the answer for everything</u>.

— (Ecclesiastes 10:19 NIV)

Up until today, you just saw money as money, but it's the one seed that can answer almost every need, dream and desire if you know how to use it skillfully. Just like a natural seed has a name, your money must also be assigned a name when it's planted in good soil. You call it money, but God calls it a seed. When you begin to think about money the way your Heavenly Father does, then the prison doors of lack and poverty have no choice but to be opened for you, and you will step into financial abundance. You have been given the power to create an abundant life beyond anything you could ever ask or think and it has been hidden, up until today, in the seed! Your power lies in first knowing money is just a seed then in knowing how to sow it to produce an "expected harvest." Remember seed lying on the table or in your pocket, will never produce a harvest.

Now he who supplies seed to the sower and bread for food will also supply and increase your store of seed and will enlarge the harvest of your righteousness. You will be enriched in every way so that you can be generous on every occasion, and through us your generosity will result in thanksgiving to God.

— (2 Corinthians 9:10, 11 NIV)

If you go back and read this chapter, you'll find Paul encouraging the Corinthians to be generous with their MONEY. The Bible says God supplies seed to the sower, not every Christian or every person who attends church services. He only gives it to the sower. Being a sower is an occupation. It's no different than being a doctor or a lawyer who practices in their field. Their occupation is how they make their living. It's also their calling. My friend, you are called to be a sower. Sowing must become your occupation from this day forward because it's the only way you will make a "life" for yourself and your household. So, right now, by a move in the spirit, if you accept this key, go ahead and write sower on your spiritual resume.

In **2 Corinthians**, Paul was talking about money being used as a seed. Your money is nothing but a seed, therefore when you sow it, you must give it a name in the same way a natural seed has a name. You must also be specific with the name you give your seed. When you pick up a pack of apple seed, it will state the exact kind of apples it will produce. This is how you have to handle your money seed; it must be given a specific and exact name to produce an expected harvest. God doesn't supply houses, cars and jobs; He only supplies **house seed**, **car seed** and **job seed**. Anything else would be a violation to the law He established in the beginning- the law of seedtime and harvest. Everything in this earth must come through a seed. Renew your mind where money is concerned. Say it out loud, **"Money is nothing but a seed."**

As you look at **2 Corinthians 9:10**, also note God doesn't just supply seed but He also supplies bread for food, and increases your store of seed. What does this look like in everyday terms? God will supply money seed for you to plant into His kingdom so His will and purposes are accomplished; He will make sure you are taken care of in the process and He will ensure your store of seed continues to increase so you will have more to give into His work. This verse should bring freedom to you in the area of giving, because your Father has everything covered. This seed principle is perpetual, meaning it continues as long as you want to stay in the cycle. But, God only makes this promise available for the sower.

Just like the natural realm, the weather conditions may not look that great when you sow, but you have to keep on sowing, knowing your harvest must manifest. If you can't let your money seed go, then I am not talking to you. But if you are willing to be rich toward God, and use the money for its intended purpose, then He will enrich you in every way, so He can be glorified. What's the purpose? To be blessed to be a blessing until all nations of the earth are blessed. The only way to accomplish this is to use your money as a seed.

Don't Hate The Messenger

Maybe you've heard someone teach about money being a seed before, but thought it was some old "prosperity preaching." Well it is! Your God is a God of prosperity. He is an extravagant God! There are some who haven't heard this good news of the gospel because there aren't enough men and women of God teaching the body how to plant financial seed and reap an intended harvest. On the other hand, those whom God has raised up to teach in this area have suffered a great deal of persecution- mainly from the church. It puts me in mind of a statement Jesus made to the people of Jerusalem.

"Jerusalem, Jerusalem, you who kill the prophets and stone those sent to you, how often I have longed to gather your children together, as a hen gathers her chicks under her wings, and you were not willing.

— (Matthew 23:37 NIV)

You see, we cry out to God for help and when He sends a deliverer we want to kill and stone the messenger. We post all kinds of negative stuff about the man or woman of God on Facebook and agree with preachers who bash them publicly, calling them false prophets and "prosperity preachers"; but we still don't have our money! We say, "All they talk about is money,"

Apostle Leroy Thompson is one of the most powerful men of God I can think of who teaches in the financial arena. He is nothing short of a modern day Abraham. He has laid the foundation for years and endured much persecution for doing so, but God has raised him up as a trailblazer in the area of financial abundance and overflow. This mighty man of God has found out and is teaching, that money is nothing but a seed, and his lifestyle testifies to this truth. I have been partners with his ministry for several years and have been blessed beyond my dreams but as far as I am concerned God has only just begun. The more I listen to his sermons, the more revelation the Holy Spirit imparts to me and the higher the Lord continues to take me financially. This is a man you will love or hate for the message he brings. Sometimes the message will cut you like a knife, but it will also bring healing and deliverance if you'll receive it. I would highly encourage you to begin reading his books and listening to his sermons on **http://eiwm.org**. Your life will never be the same!

The deliverers have been sent out but you can't hate the messenger. They have been dispatched to your area in response to your prayers. Get ready to put your pride aside and allow the Word of God, spoken through these mighty men and women of God to break you out of poverty into financial abundance.

What's In Your Seed?

If I held up an apple seed in front of someone and asked what they see, most people would respond "an apple seed." They can't see the tree- just the seed in their hand. But we should be able to see the tree by looking at the seed. This is called foresight. This means you look forward into the future and see the finished product. Isn't that what faith is all about? If you really have faith you should see the finished product just like your Heavenly Father sees the beginning from the end and the end from the beginning- Isaiah 46:10.

Here's another example of faith when it truly sees.

"Have faith in God," Jesus answered. "Truly I tell you, if anyone says to this mountain, 'Go, throw yourself into the sea,' and does not doubt in their heart but believes that what they say will happen, it will be done for them. Therefore I tell you, whatever you ask for in prayer, believe that you have received it, and it will be yours.

— (Mark 11:23-24 NIV)

In the verses above, Jesus said believe you **HAVE RECEIVED**. He didn't say anything about say, "I'm believing I am going to get what I prayed for." Get that word, (believing), out of your vocabulary if you intend to break out of poverty into financial abundance! On the contrary, Mark said you have to **believe you have already received what you ask for WHEN you pray, not after it shows up!** This means when I pray over my seed or for any situation, I have to walk away like I already have it. When I teach I always say, "You won't see it until you see it." If you can't see yourself debt free, if you can't see yourself in your new home, if you can't see yourself breaking out of poverty into financial abundance before it manifests, then you will never see it in the natural.

When you hold a one hundred dollar bill in your hand what do you see? Does your vision go beyond the one hundred dollar bill? Do you see it as all you have? The same way we talked about looking at the natural seed and seeing the end product is the same you have to start looking at your money seed. When you sow your money seed, you should see the harvest the moment it's planted in the soil. That should give you a reason to rejoice.

Do you remember the widow with her jar of oil in the book of Kings?

The wife of a man from the company of the prophets cried out to Elisha, "Your servant my husband is dead, and you know that he revered the Lord. But now his creditor is coming to take my two boys as his slaves." Elisha replied to her, "How can I help you? Tell me, what do you have in your house?""Your servant has nothing there at all," she said, "except a small jar of olive oil."Elisha said, "Go around and ask all your neighbors for empty jars. Don't ask for just a few. Then go inside and shut the door behind you and your sons. Pour oil into all the jars, and as each is

filled, put it to one side." She left him and shut the door behind her and her sons. They brought the jars to her and she kept pouring. When all the jars were full, she said to her son, "Bring me another one." But he replied, "There is not a jar left." Then the oil stopped flowing. She went and told the man of God, and he said, "Go, sell the oil and pay your debts. You and your sons can live on what is left."

— (2 Kings 4:1-4 NIV)

This widow didn't know how powerful her seed was. She just saw a jar of oil, but God saw total debt freedom and enough money for her and her family to live on for the rest of their lives! It's time for you to start seeing the potential of your seed. Start looking at your money as a seed to bless the kingdom of God, to bless others and to live the God kind of life you have always dreamed of.

For the record, your dreams will never be fulfilled through your J.O.B. No matter how hard you work or how many jobs you have, you will never live the life you want through the secular system. Your job was given to you as a place to get your **seed**. It's not your source of sustenance; it's just a channel God uses to get your seed to you.

On another note, don't let people outside of the kingdom trick you into believing they have it better than you do. How many sports figures, singers and Hollywood stars have you seen go bankrupt? A whole lot! Many of them are living from paycheck to paycheck, they're just doing it on a higher level. Don't let them fool you. If you want to prosper and have success, then start seeing your money as a seed and start working kingdom financial principles. Say this with me, "my money is nothing but a seed." Some people have more seed than others, depending upon how well they did with the last batch they had.

He who is faithful in a very little [thing] is faithful also in much, and he who is dishonest and unjust in a very little [thing] is dishonest and unjust also in much. Therefore if you have not been faithful in the [case of] unrighteous mammon (deceitful riches, money, possessions), who will entrust to you the true riches? And if you have not proved faithful in that which belongs to another [whether God or man], who will give you that which is your own [that is, the true riches]?

— (Luke 16:10-12 AMP)

Your faithfulness with the seed you have been given will determine your future supply. In order to increase your current seed account you have to show yourself faithful with what God puts in your hands.

We have established the kingdom of God is a seed based system. In order for anything in this earth to multiply it must come through a seed. You also should know now that your money is nothing but a seed. We will now pair this knowledge with your money seed and find out how you can create the life more abundantly Jesus intended for you to have.

Chapter 13

How To Skillfully Sow Your Seed

If you made it this far, you might as well go ahead and pack your bags because you are just a few minutes away from walking out of the prison of poverty into a world of financial abundance. This chapter holds the master key on how to sow your seed and reap an intended and expected harvest every single time. We are going to tie together everything we've learned up to this point right here in this chapter.

Steps To Reaping Your Harvest

1. Return Your Tithe To The Storehouse

Don't withhold your tithe. Remember it doesn't belong

to you. You have not sown an offering seed until you have returned the tithe to your storehouse. Rejection of this step negates the other steps which follow.

2. Decide Your Harvest- Name Your Seed

Money seed can be assigned any name. As long as it's in alignment with the Word of God and the plan He has for your life, then you will reap the harvest. For example you may say, "I want to sow to be a millionaire," but if that's not part of God's plan for your assignment you will not receive the harvest. When you sow your seed be **VERY specific**. For example you would not sow for financial increase. That could be $1! You could name the seed for a $5,000 harvest. You could also sow a seed for a job. Be specific about the type of job, benefits you expect to have etc.

For our example, let's say you want to reap a harvest of $5,000.

3. Identify The Seed

Ask the Holy Spirit what seed you need to sow to produce the $5,000 harvest. He is the teacher of profit Isa. 48:17. He's the only one who can identify the correct seed. Remember, the wrong seed in the right soil will not produce the expected harvest.

4. Identify The Right Soil

Your seed **must** go into good soil. The right seed in the wrong soil will still yield zero results. Don't assume the seed needs to be sown at your current church. You might be instructed to sow it into another ministry or into the life of a particular person. The Holy Spirit has to tell you where to sow the seed. All you have to do is obey Him. Don't second guess Him or try to rationalize what He tells you to do.

5. Pray Over Your Seed

Once you have your seed declare **Mark 11:23-24** over it. Here is an example of how to pray over your seed: **Father your Word says when I pray to believe I have received and I will have what I have asked for. Therefore, as I plant this seed in good soil, I decree and declare I receive right now by faith my harvest of $5,000 in the name of Jesus (in the authority found in Jesus' name).**

6. See Your Harvest /Put Your Faith On It And Walk Off

Once you've prayed over your seed, plant it where you have been instructed. Just put your faith on it and walk away just like Jesus did with the fig tree. He didn't stand around waiting for the fig tree to die. He already saw the tree withered up and dead when He spoke the Word to it. When you sow, see your harvest not the seed. Get your eyes off of the visible provision onto the invisible.

7. Thank God For The Harvest

How does a person act who believes they have **already received** their harvest? Do they walk away somber and sad? God says He loves a cheerful giver. That's a person who is hilarious and happy when he or she gives. You should act like you just received what you sowed and prayed for if you really "see it" and have received it. Thank God in a loud and boisterous manner because you just received. From that day forward continue to thank Him for the harvest until it manifests.

About two months ago I planted a $100 seed and the Holy Spirit told me to believe for a $10,000 harvest. By the way, sometimes God will tell you the seed to sow and the harvest to expect. After I planted the seed, boy I had a praise fest because as far as I was concerned I had already received the $10,000 harvest! The next day my harvest started coming in through contracts from my business. Within a few weeks I had identified my $10,000 harvest, but I had to work for it because it came through contracts. It came in "pieces"; Your harvest may not come in at one time or through the same source. Be wise and watch as it comes in or you'll eat it up and swear this doesn't work.

8. Be Ready For Opportunities, Ideas And Instruction

In the example I gave you above, my harvest came through my

business. I was given the opportunity through contracts but I had to make sure the work got done or there wouldn't have been a harvest. Your harvest may come through a "process." There may be a few steps you'll have to take to receive it. It may come a little at a time. Be sensitive to the Holy Spirit and EXPECT an idea, opportunity or instruction to show up. This is a very critical step in the process and one of the reasons many fail to reap their harvest. Look for it and act upon it!

9. Don't Dig Up Your Seed

Earlier in this book we talked about the importance of your words and thoughts. This is where the testing of your faith is at the most critical stage. It's during the "time" stage most people abort their harvest.

They begin to say things to cancel out what they believed they received. For example, if you sowed a seed for a new car and start saying "I don't know how I'm going to get a car", or "It looks like I'll be walking for a while because I can't afford a new car," you might as well call it a day because you are not going to get the car. You just dug up your seed. Look at what James said.

But when you ask, you must believe and not doubt, because the one who doubts is like a wave of the sea,

blown and tossed by the wind. <u>That person should not</u>
<u>expect to receive anything from the Lord.</u> Such a person
is double-minded and unstable in all they do.

— (James 1:6-8 NIV)

The only water your seed will respond to is the Word of God.
If you speak anything concerning your harvest, it better be
the Word, and it better include thanksgiving. Anything else
will cause you to abort your harvest and you'll think the seed
system doesn't work. I promise you it works if you work it.

10. Don't Eat Your Seed!

Don't eat your seed! Remember God doesn't give houses,
cars and land; He gives seed to the sower. Don't make the
fatal mistake of eating your seed. You might be asking for a
job but God will give you a job seed. So be careful.

11. Keep The Cycle Going

When a farmer reaps his harvest, he doesn't stash everything
away and say "oh well, I got my harvest and I am satisfied."
If he took this approach with his harvest, he and his family
would find themselves in the place most Christians are in-
not enough, lack and insufficiency. You have to be wise when
your harvest comes in. Don't eat your seed! Before you go
running off to pay your bills, or go shopping for the new car
with your increase, the first thing you should do is remove

the tithe, then ask the Holy Spirit how much seed needs to be sown. If this isn't done, you will find yourself right back where you started.

As mentioned before, sowing creates a perpetual harvest as long as you are willing to stay in the loop. Sowing only when you have a need will produce a very stressful life and you'll find yourself going from one financial problem to the next. Can you imagine if the farmers across the nation only sowed when they thought you were hungry? You would starve to death and die! This is what's happening to us financially. It's time to move from need to need sowing and be translated from glory to glory in the area of our finances! If you continue sowing you'll find harvests showing up on every turn and abundance will overtake you.

If you apply these eleven principles every time you sow your seed, your days of just enough and paycheck to paycheck living are over. You might as well declare, **"I am out of poverty and am walking in financial abundance!"**

Let me add one more thing before I close this chapter. Count this as a bonus: Don't get hung up on the amount of the seed. I could have gotten hung up on a $100 seed for a $10,000 harvest because that really is a small amount to sow for $10,000! Don't get tripped up by how small or large your seed is. Just obey God. The Bible tells us not to despise small beginnings.

Though thy beginning was small, yet thy latter end should greatly increase.

— **(Job 8:7 KJV)**

If you obey the Holy Spirit in your giving, your latter end will not only increase, but greatly increase. You'll find yourself going from a $5 seed to $20 to $100 to $1,000 and so on just like I did. I started out with $8 but today it's not uncommon for me to sow several thousand dollars at the conferences I attend; but I didn't start out that way. Don't ever say your seed is not much, I tell you the truth, my $8 seed has come a long way! A $5 seed is just as powerful and as precious to God as a $1,000 seed when it's directed by the Holy Spirit.

He that goeth forth and weepeth, <u>bearing precious seed</u>, shall doubtless come again with rejoicing, bringing his sheaves with him.

— **(Psalm 126:6 KJV)**

Your seed is precious to God. Say what He says about it and you will doubtless or will without a doubt come again with rejoicing, bringing in your harvest. Praise God! You have just opened the doors of your financial prison. Welcome to financial abundance!

***WARNING** Remember Satan will come immediately to steal the Word you have planted in your heart. You are armed with life changing revelation so don't think the enemy is going to bow out gracefully and allow you to break free from financial bondage. You will have to pass the money test. You will have to be able to overcome the temptation of Satan who will apply pressure on you to give up your keys of abundance.

Chapter 14

Maintaining Abundance Through The Law of Love

In 2011 my seed brought in a beautiful 2011 Jaguar XF for an unbelievable price; but once I had the car I understood maintenance was going to be required. Gas has to be put in the car for it to run and it needs to be washed on a bi- weekly basis. The oil needs to be checked and so on. From time to time, I pull out my car manual to check when it's time for each service. In the same manner, we have to pull out our manual of life as well. We need to stay in the Word of God and check ourselves so we'll continue to walk in love. Perform a maintenance check-up on your life every day to ensure you are walking in the law of love. You can give away millions of dollars, but if you don't walk in love, you'll eventually lose what you've been given. God blesses the righteous- those who hold fast to God's way of doing and being right. Your seed won't reach its full potential if you're not walking in love with your husband, wife, children, employer, etc.

One of them, an expert in the law, tested him with this question: "Teacher, which is the greatest commandment in the Law?" Jesus replied: "'Love the Lord your God with all your heart and with all your soul and with all your mind.' This is the first and greatest commandment. And the second is like it: 'Love your neighbor as yourself.' <u>All the Law and the Prophets hang on these two commandments</u>."

— (Matthew 22:37-40 NIV)

Everything in the Word of God is motivated by and hangs on the law of love. In John, Jesus gave us a new commandment to love one another. Make it your business to maintain a lifestyle of walking in love, if you want to continue experiencing the abundant life God has for you. This isn't always easy, but it's doable. My grandmother used to say, "God don't like ugly." Now I know she meant He expected me to walk in the perfect law of love.

"Therefore, if you are offering your gift at the altar and there remember that your brother or sister has something against you, leave your gift there in front of the altar. First go and be reconciled to them; then come and offer your gift.

— (Matthew 5:23-24 NIV)

Jesus said, if you know someone who is holding something against you, **leave your offering** at the altar and go be reconciled to your brother or sister. Now, if they don't want to be reconciled after you make the attempt, that's ok; you have done what Jesus commanded you to do. It's up to them to get their heart right before God. He knew the offering wasn't going to be acceptable to the Father, if the perfect law of love wasn't at work. Do you know why everything must hang on love? Jesus commanded us to love; God is love; and your faith works by love.

For in Jesus Christ neither circumcision availeth any thing, nor uncircumcision; but faith which worketh by love.

— (Galatians 5:6 KJV)

Whoever does not love does not know God, because God is love.

— (1 John 4:8 NIV)

You will stay out of the prison of poverty and maintain abundance when you walk in love. Let love be the motivation behind everything you do.

Chapter 15

Make Your Money Work For you

In **Matthew twenty-five verses fifteen through thirty**, Jesus told a parable about three men who were stewards over different increments of money- five, two and one talent. By the way Matthew twenty - five is not about "singing and dancing" talents; it's about money. When the man returned he wanted to settle accounts with each steward. Each one did well except for the one who was entrusted with the one talent.

Then he which had received the one talent came and said, Lord, I knew thee that thou art an hard man, reaping where thou hast not sown, and gathering where thou hast not strawed: And I was afraid, and went and hid

thy talent in the earth: lo, there thou hast that is thine. His lord answered and said unto him, Thou wicked and slothful servant, thou knewest that I reap where I sowed not, and gather where I have not strawed: Thou oughtest therefore to have put my money to the exchangers, and then at my coming I should have received mine own with usury. Take therefore the talent from him, and give it unto him which hath ten talents.

— (Matthew 25: 24-28 KJV)

God expects us to put our money to work for His kingdom. He told the unjust servant, you could have at least put the money in the bank so I could get some interest. Interest from the bank was the least he expected! God is a God of multiplication- that's all He's interested in. He wants to know what you did with the financial resources He has given you.

Today we take our money and put it into 401k plans which we can't touch for twenty to thirty years without a penalty. Some employers offer the employee the opportunity to borrow a percentage of their own money and charge them interest to pay themselves back! What kind of system is that? Now, if you have a 401k I am not saying you shouldn't have one. I will say this; all of your money shouldn't be in one basket. What if something happens to your employer and they go out of business? I have had many clients tell me they lost their money in an employer sponsored 401k program. I'm not trying to create fear, but I want you to be aware of a better way to multiply your money and be able to have access to it.

A good investment is one which you are able to liquidate without a penalty when you need the funds. An example of this could be stocks, gold and silver, real estate, land; even some annuities allow you to take out a portion of the money. Though the stock market is a bit volatile, there's still money to be made for those who do their homework and are led by the Holy Spirit in their investing.

One of the areas I believe is critical for every Christian to invest in is gold and silver. God doesn't print paper money. Remember it's just a seed. True wealth is in land, property, gold and silver. God is the one who put the gold in the earth- so this is true wealth. We should have already had a real wake-up call when the world's economy went into recession a few years ago. Notice I said the world's economy, because we are part of the kingdom economy and God is never in recession!

If you check this out for yourself, you'll find the value of the dollar has been on a decline for quite some time and I believe we are going to hit another very critical point again in the next seven years. The dollar will be worth far less than we have ever seen before. I base this upon my own study, my connection with an expert in this industry who says the same thing and a guest I recently saw on the Sid Roth show named Shane Warren. Mr. Warren received an open vision from God showing him what was going to happen to the economy in the near future. One of the major things that occurred was the devaluing of the dollar. We have to get our head out of the sand and use worldly wealth to accumulate kingdom wealth. Paper money is not wealth, it's a seed. I believe God is giving us an opportunity to hedge ourselves in before this difficult time arrives. God says,

'The silver is mine and the gold is mine,' declares the Lord Almighty."

— (Haggai 2:8 NIV)

And Abram was very rich in cattle, in silver, and in gold.
— (Genesis 13:2 NIV)

Abram wasn't rich in credit lines, loans and paper money. Paper money and credit is the "world's" medium of exchange. If you get tied up in credit lines and loans, a time is going to come when the world's system will deteriorate to such a severe state they'll call in those loans and credit lines. When they do, some folks are going to be in for a big surprise. Spend the next few years getting out of debt and putting your seed to work by investing in gold ,silver real estate, etc.

Gold or silver in your mutual fund portfolio is not the same as owning gold and silver. I'm talking about having the hard asset or a certificate of deposit which shows you actually own it. How do you know the gold or silver in your stock or mutual fund portfolio is really there? It's really just on paper. Ask them to send it to you or give you a certificate showing it's on deposit in your name. It'll never happen! You might think I am being a bit skeptical about our financial system, but if you've been around for some time you should know everything that glitters isn't gold- no pun intended. You saw what happened with the banks and investment companies didn't you? I personally hold these hard assets. When I started investing in gold and silver I had no idea what I was doing, but now I do.

The Father expects you to take your seed (money) and invest it wisely. I would like to encourage you to begin investing in kingdom wealth- gold, silver, land, houses and even cattle. If you would like to get more information on how to start investing in gold and silver please visit the website below to receive your free packet: **http://christiangoldsilver.com**.

Chapter 16

Tither's Declaration

Whenever you return your tithe to your storehouse, a blessing (words) should be spoken over it. Even if they do this at your church, take the time to declare the Word of God over your tithe and offering. Don't ever just take it to church and chuck it in a basket. When you declare the Word over your tithe and offering, you release your faith along with it. This is what many call, "tithing the tithe." When you sow your offering go back to chapter thirteen and follow those steps. Don't rely on anyone else to speak a blessing on your behalf.

Declaration

As I return the tithe I decree and declare I have removed God's sacred portion from amongst my own things. Therefore I decree and declare the windows of heaven are opened unto me and my household and the Father has poured out favor, goodness, wellness, health and prosperity so much so, that we don't have room enough to receive it. Thank you Father for rebuking the devourer for our sake. I decree and declare all nations call us blessed and there will be no more aborted things in our life from this day forward.

When you return the tithe and plant your offering say, "**I receive.**" See the Lord Jesus receiving your tithe and offering and making the great exchange with you! Now, begin to rejoice and thank your Father!

Praise God! You have broken out of poverty into Financial Abundance!

Invitation To Become
a Kingdom Citizen

Are you part of the kingdom of God? If not I would love to invite you to enter in today. God is looking for sons and daughters who will be led by His Spirit and take the blessing all over the earth. In order to partake in the kingdom you must come through the door He has provided- Jesus Christ.

Jesus said in

John 14:6 "I am the way and the truth and the life. No one comes to the Father except through me.

John 10: 7-9

Jesus therefore said unto them again, Verily, verily, I say unto you, I am the door of the sheep. All that came before me are thieves and robbers: but the sheep did not hear them. I am the door; by me if any man enter in, he shall be saved, and shall go in and go out, and shall find pasture.

The Lord Jesus Christ is the **ONLY** way into the kingdom of God. He has an awesome plan for your life if you will receive Him!

Romans 10: 9-13 (NIV)

If you declare with your mouth, "Jesus is Lord," and believe in your heart that God raised him from the dead, you will be saved. For it is with your heart that you believe and are justified, and it is with your mouth that you profess your faith and are saved. As Scripture says, "Anyone who believes in him will never be put to shame." For there is no difference between Jew and Gentile—the same Lord is Lord of all and richly blesses all who call on him, for, "Everyone who calls on the name of the Lord will be saved."

Pray This Prayer Out Loud

Heavenly Father, I believe Jesus Christ is the way into your kingdom. I believe Jesus died on the cross for my sins and was raised from the dead for me. He paid the price for my past, present and future sin. Therefore, I confess with my mouth Jesus is Lord of my life and believe in my heart God the Father raised Him from the dead. Jesus is now my Lord and I am saved.

Welcome to the kingdom of God! I would love to hear from you if you made Jesus your Lord and Savior!

lifeintheword@aol.com

ABOUT THE AUTHOR

Born in Paterson, New Jersey, Sonya L. Thompson currently resides in Florida and is a successful entrepreneur. She is involved in the telemarketing, vending, and financial services industries. Sonya holds a B.S. in the field of Business Administration and is a Servant Leader at Hope International Church in Groveland, Florida under Pastor Tony McCoy. She has appeared on "With God You Will Succeed" with prominent business man and speaker, Dr. Tom Leding. Sonya has also appeared for a financial segment on Afrotainment TV.

She has spoken and continues to speak at many entrepreneurial venues. Sonya has been a Christian for 21 years and has a passion to share the " Living Word", especially in the area of finances, with the body of Christ. Her calling is to "Train, Educate and Advise through the Gospel with Simplicity and Purity."

Other Books By Sonya L. Thompson

Business By The Bible

Seeds Of Prosperity Book & CD

To Order Visit:

http://lifeinthewordministries.org

Feel free to send your prayer requests and comments

22101488R00085

Made in the USA
Charleston, SC
11 September 2013